AI-POWERED PRODUCTIVITY AND CREATIVITY

Your Guide to Transforming Every Aspect of Your Life

Bo Zhang

ISBN-13: 9798865100805

Cover design by: Art Painter
Library of Congress Control Number: 2018675309
Printed in the United States of America

CHAPTER 1: GETTING STARTED WITH AI

CHAPTER 2: AI IN THE WORKPLACE

CHAPTER 3: AI FOR EDUCATION

CHAPTER 4: AI IN HEALTHCARE

CHAPTER 5: AI IN CREATIVITY

5.1. AI-Powered Content Generation for Writers and Marketers

5.2. Digital Art and Design Tools

5.3. Music Composition and Production with AI

5.4. AI-Enhanced Video and Photography Editing

CHAPTER 6: AI IN ENTERTAINMENT AND LEISURE

6.1. AI-Powered Recommendation Engines for Movies, Music, and Books

6.2. Virtual Reality and Augmented Reality Experiences

6.3. Gaming with AI-Generated Content

6.4. AI in Sports Analysis and Coaching

CHAPTER 7: AI FOR PERSONAL DEVELOPMENT

7.1. Personalized Fitness and Nutrition Recommendations

7.2. Mindfulness and Mental Health Applications

7.3. AI-Driven Personal Finance and Investment Advice

CHAPTER 8: PRIVACY AND ETHICS IN AI

CHAPTER 9: THE FUTURE OF AI

9.1. Emerging Trends and Cutting-Edge AI Innovations

9.2. Preparing for the AI-Driven World of Tomorrow

CHAPTER 10: BUILDING YOUR OWN AI PROJECTS

AI-POWERED PRODUCTIVITY AND CREATIVITY

Your Guide to Transforming Every Aspect of Your Life

INTRODUCTION

Welcome to the thrilling world of AI technology, where productivity and creativity flourish like never before! The advent of Artificial Intelligence (AI) has been a game-changer, especially in the past 5 to 10 years, redefining our human potential in remarkable ways. As we navigate this dynamic landscape, AI products and services have emerged as powerful tools, ready to assist us in elevating various aspects of our lives. This guidebook is your open door to understanding the AI revolution, discovering advanced products and applications, recognizing its profound impact on our world, and learning how to harness its capabilities to transform your life.

The story of AI began with a quest to replicate human intelligence in machines, but it's grown into something far more extraordinary. Over time, AI has transcended the realm of science fiction, seamlessly integrating into our daily existence. It's the magic behind the scenes, powering algorithms that guide our online shopping recommendations, revolutionizing healthcare through diagnostics, and infusing creativity into content generation and design. It's the wizardry behind search engines, the autonomy of vehicles, and the magic of virtual personal assistants.

AI's influence has permeated every corner of our world, showcasing its boundless potential. Not only has it streamlined the way we work, but it has also enriched our leisure time. It's transforming education, making healthcare more accessible and efficient, and sparking innovation in our creative pursuits. In essence, AI is the driving force behind a modern-day Renaissance.

In a world that's in perpetual motion, keeping up with technological advancements is essential. The rise of AI is no exception. As AI continues to advance, its presence in our lives is poised to expand even further. It's no longer the domain of tech wizards; it's a necessity for professionals, students, artists, and anyone seeking to be more efficient, creative, and successful.

The future of AI is brimming with promise. We're standing on the edge of groundbreaking innovations, from quantum AI to brain-computer interfaces, and they're set to reshape our world in ways we can't yet imagine. These innovations will lead us into a future where the ordinary is transformed into the extraordinary.

This guidebook is your personal key to unlock the boundless possibilities AI has to offer. It's a practical resource, designed to equip you with knowledge and insights to navigate this ever-evolving landscape. Whether you're a newcomer to the world of AI or a passionate enthusiast, the practical advice, real-world examples, and valuable tips found within will empower you to harness AI's full potential. As you embark on this thrilling journey through the realms of AI, consider this guidebook your steadfast companion, ready to help you embrace the future and revolutionize your life.

CHAPTER 1: GETTING STARTED WITH AI

Welcome to the first step in your AI journey. In this chapter, we'll lay the foundation for your exploration of the AI landscape. We'll begin by understanding the building blocks of AI and delving into the basics of machine learning and neural networks. You'll discover how these fundamental concepts power the AI applications you encounter daily.

But before we dive deeper, we'll address some common misconceptions about AI. It's essential to clear the air and dispel any myths that might be hindering your understanding or progress in this field.

Once we've established a solid understanding of the AI fundamentals, we'll move on to practical matters. We'll guide you through setting up your AI environment, ensuring that you have the tools and resources necessary to embark on your AI journey. From software choices to hardware considerations, we'll help you make the right decisions, tailored to your specific needs.

So, let's begin with the basics, debunk myths, and equip you with the tools you need to take your first steps into the fascinating world of AI.

1.1. Understanding the Basics: Machine Learning and Neural Networks

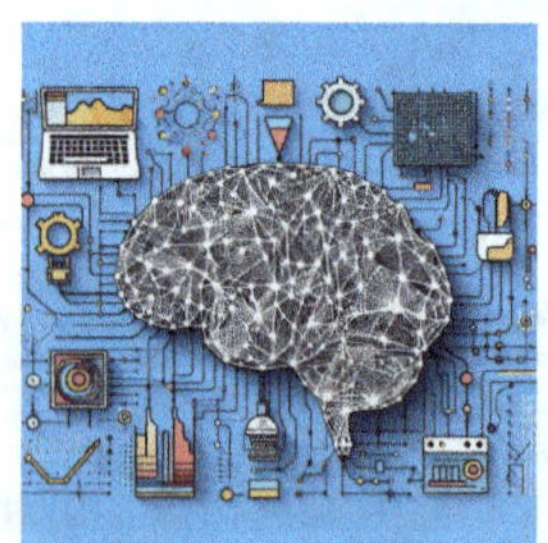

At the heart of the AI revolution lies the remarkable field of machine learning, and within it, a powerful concept known as neural networks. In this section, we will unravel the core principles of machine learning and the workings of neural networks to provide you with a solid foundation for your AI journey.

Machine Learning: The Brains Behind AI

Machine learning is the driving force behind AI's transformative power. It's the technology that enables machines to learn from data, recognize patterns, make predictions, and improve their performance over time without being explicitly programmed. Think of it as teaching a computer to think, reason, and adapt, much like the human brain but with a penchant for analyzing massive datasets at lightning speed.

There are several types of machine learning, each with its own unique characteristics. Here are a few of the most common:

- **Supervised Learning**: In this approach, the machine is fed labeled data, meaning it's provided with input-output pairs, and its task is to learn the mapping from inputs to outputs. This is the basis for tasks like image recognition, language translation, and much more. Imagine it as training a computer to recognize cats in pictures by showing it many cat images labeled as "cat."

- **Unsupervised Learning**: This type of learning involves exposing the machine to unlabeled data and asking it to discover patterns or structures within the data. It's often used in clustering, where the machine groups data points that are similar to one another, or dimensionality reduction, where it simplifies complex data while retaining its essence. Unsupervised learning might be like showing the computer a mix of animals and asking it to identify groups without knowing which are cats or dogs in advance.

- ***Reinforcement Learning***: Here, machines learn through interaction with an environment. They make decisions, take actions, and receive feedback in the form of rewards or penalties. This approach is prevalent in robotics and game playing. Think of it as training a robot to play chess; it makes moves and learns from winning or losing the game.

- ***Deep Learning***: Deep learning is a subfield of machine learning that focuses on artificial neural networks, particularly deep neural networks with multiple layers. Deep learning has revolutionized the field and is responsible for many of the incredible advancements in AI we see today. Deep neural networks are like a more complex version of our brain's neural connections and are particularly good at recognizing patterns in data.

Neural Networks: The Mimicry of the Brain

Neural networks, inspired by the human brain, are the fundamental building blocks of deep learning and have played a pivotal role in many AI breakthroughs. They consist of interconnected layers of nodes, or artificial neurons, each of which processes and transmits information.

In a neural network, data is fed into the input layer, processed through multiple hidden layers, and produces an output. The strength of neural networks lies in their ability to automatically discover intricate patterns and relationships within data. From recognizing images and speech to predicting stock market trends, neural networks excel at a vast array of tasks.

As you dive deeper into the world of AI, understanding the principles of machine learning and neural networks will empower you to comprehend how AI systems function and why they are so incredibly adept at various tasks. Armed with this knowledge, you'll be well-prepared to explore the myriad applications of AI in the chapters that follow. You'll not only use AI but also appreciate the fascinating complexity that makes it all possible.

1.2. Common Misconceptions about AI

As the technology develops, AI has been

shrouded in a few common misconceptions that warrant our attention. If left unaddressed, these misunderstandings can hinder a clear understanding of artificial intelligence. Let's explore these misconceptions, offering real-world examples to illuminate their realities.

AI Possesses Human-Like Understanding

Some imagine AI as a technological entity with a profound, human-like comprehension of the world. They envision thinking, feeling, and grasping concepts in a manner akin to human beings. In reality, AI, as it stands today, lacks consciousness, emotions, and the ability to understand the world as humans do. It doesn't experience emotions or thoughts in the way humans do. Instead, AI operates on the basis of data and algorithms. For example, AI can recognize spoken language and provide appropriate responses, but it doesn't truly understand language. It lacks genuine emotions, even if it can discern and respond to emotional cues in text or speech.

AI Can Replace Humans Completely

There's a fear that AI might lead to the displacement of human workers across various industries, causing widespread job losses. The truth is that while AI can automate specific tasks and enhance efficiency, it is essentially a tool designed to augment human abilities rather than replace them. In manufacturing, for instance, robots and AI-driven machines can assemble products, but humans are indispensable for designing new products, maintaining machinery, and making strategic decisions. AI complements human intelligence and is most adept at handling repetitive, data-driven tasks, allowing humans to focus on more creative and complex endeavors.

AI Understands Everything About Data

It's a common misconception that AI comprehends all facets of data, making it infallible in decision-making. In reality, AI's understanding is confined to the data on which it has been trained. For example, a machine learning model trained on medical data can diagnose diseases based on the patterns it has learned, but it may not consider external factors or unforeseen data. If the training data is incomplete or biased, AI can make errors. Inaccurate or biased training data can lead to erroneous results.

AI Is Infallible and Unbiased

Some believe that AI is perpetually accurate and devoid of biases, ensuring fair and just decisions. In fact, AI's performance is as good as the quality of the data on which it relies.

For instance, a facial recognition system trained mostly on images of one racial group may perform poorly on other racial groups, leading to biased outcomes. It's imperative to monitor and fine-tune AI systems to mitigate biases and inaccuracies.

All AI Is Superintelligent

AI is often depicted in popular media as highly intelligent, surpassing human cognition. The truth is that most AI in use today is narrow or weak AI. While it can excel at specific tasks, it lacks the general intelligence found in humans. For example, AI can outperform humans in chess or go, but it doesn't possess the broad spectrum of cognitive abilities that humans exhibit.

AI Can Think Creatively

There's a belief that AI can generate entirely original, creative ideas, much like human artists or writers. In practice, AI can produce creative content but relies on patterns and data. For instance, it can generate artwork, poetry, or music based on patterns it has learned from existing works. However, it doesn't possess the same depth of creativity, intuition, or emotional connection as humans.

Addressing these misconceptions is essential for approaching AI with a clear and informed perspective. While AI is a potent tool, understanding its capabilities and limitations is crucial for harnessing its potential in various aspects of life.

1.3. Setting Up Your AI Environment

Starting your journey in artificial intelligence is an exciting step, but before you can dive into the world of AI development, you need to set up the right environment. In this section, we'll guide you through the process, breaking it down into manageable steps to ensure that even readers without prior AI knowledge can understand and follow along. We'll cover everything from your choice of operating system to hardware considerations and cloud-based options, giving you a holistic view of the AI environment.

1. Choose Your Operating System

Let's begin with your choice of operating system. Just as a painter selects a canvas, you'll need to pick the right foundation for your AI work. Most AI frameworks and tools are compatible with three major operating systems: Windows, macOS, and Linux. Your selection here depends on your familiarity and comfort with a particular operating system. For AI development, Linux, especially distributions like Ubuntu, is favored by many due to its robust support and compatibility with AI libraries.

2. Python: The Lingua Franca of AI

Now, imagine Python as the language of communication between you and your AI tools. It's the lingua franca of AI and for a good reason. Python offers an extensive ecosystem of libraries and frameworks, making it indispensable for AI development. Think of Python as your canvas, and libraries like TensorFlow, PyTorch, and scikit-learn as the paints you'll use to create your AI masterpiece. Ensure you have Python installed on your system, preferably in its latest version, and consider using a Python virtual environment to manage your AI projects cleanly.

3. AI Libraries and Frameworks

These libraries and frameworks are your toolset. They provide you with pre-built functions and tools for AI development. Whether you're working on image recognition or natural language processing, libraries like TensorFlow, PyTorch, and Keras offer you ready-made brushes and colors to craft your AI art.

4. Integrated Development Environments (IDEs)

Think of an Integrated Development Environment (IDE) as your AI studio. It's the place where you'll write, test, and run your AI code. Jupyter Notebook, Visual Studio Code, and PyCharm are like artist studios, each offering a comfortable space for your creative process. Jupyter Notebook, in particular, is like an interactive sketchbook, favored by data scientists for its ease of use and shareable nature.

5. Hardware Considerations

AI development can be a bit like sculpting. Some projects may be simple and can be shaped with basic tools, like a pocketknife. But more complex projects might require specialized equipment. For AI, that specialized equipment can be in the form of powerful graphics processing units (GPUs) or dedicated AI accelerators like the NVIDIA Tesla series. Your choice of hardware depends on the scale and complexity of your AI projects. For beginners, standard laptops or desktops will suffice, but as your projects grow in size and complexity, you might need to invest in more powerful hardware.

6. Cloud-Based AI Services

Here's the cool part - you don't necessarily need to own your equipment. Think of cloud-based AI services as renting a state-of-the-art studio with all the tools and materials you need. Companies like Amazon Web Services (AWS), Google Cloud, and Microsoft Azure offer cloud-based AI services, pre-configured environments, and access to powerful GPUs for your AI development. It's like having access to a world-class art studio without the need to buy all the tools and equipment yourself.

7. Data Preparation and Storage

Finally, you'll need to think about your canvas and paints. AI projects often involve vast datasets, and just like a painter needs a palette and canvas, you'll need a structured system for data collection, storage, and preprocessing. Whether you use a local server or cloud-based solutions, organizing your data is essential for the success of your AI projects. It's akin to having all your art supplies neatly organized and ready to use.

By setting up your AI environment thoughtfully and systematically, you're ensuring a smooth and efficient AI development journey. These initial steps are like preparing your art studio before embarking on a grand painting; they lay the foundation for your AI adventure, enabling you to create beautiful AI art in the chapters ahead.

1.4. Choosing the Right Hardware and Software

In many cases, your choice of hardware and software can significantly influence your AI journey's success. This section serves as your guide to understanding the critical considerations when it comes to hardware and software in the AI field. We'll break down these choices into manageable sections, ensuring that both beginners and those with more advanced AI knowledge can follow along.

1. Hardware Considerations

Let's begin with the hardware component, which plays a crucial role in AI development. Consider hardware as the tools in an artist's studio - selecting the right ones can make your AI projects more efficient and effective. Here are some key considerations:

a. ***Standard Laptops and Desktops***: These are like your basic artist's canvas and brushes. For beginners or small-scale AI projects, standard laptops and desktops are perfectly suitable. You can commence your AI journey using these devices. However, for complex AI models and tasks, especially those involving deep learning, you may need more powerful hardware.

b. ***Graphics Processing Units (GPUs)***: Think of GPUs as high-quality brushes in an artist's toolkit. They are essential for tasks that involve deep learning and complex computations. GPUs are designed to process large volumes of data rapidly, making them invaluable for AI model training. Notable GPU manufacturers include NVIDIA and AMD.

c. ***AI Accelerators***: Dedicated AI accelerators, such as NVIDIA's Tesla series or Google's Tensor Processing Units (TPUs), can be likened to specialized tools for specific artistic techniques. These accelerators are designed to speed up AI workloads, particularly for deep learning tasks. They excel in performing repetitive AI computations with efficiency.

2. Software Selection

Now, let's explore the software side of the equation, which is comparable to selecting the type of paints and brushes you'll use for your art. Here's what you need to consider:

a. ***Operating System***: Your choice of operating system is akin to selecting the canvas on which you'll create your AI masterpieces. Windows, macOS, and Linux are all viable options. Many AI professionals favor Linux, particularly distributions like Ubuntu, for its compatibility and extensive support for AI libraries.

b. ***Programming Language***: Python is the language of choice for AI development. Think of it as the universal language in the art world. Most AI libraries and frameworks, such as TensorFlow,

PyTorch, and scikit-learn, are Python-based. Ensuring you have Python installed is fundamental to your AI work.

c. *AI Libraries and Frameworks*: These are the paints and brushes you use to craft your AI art. TensorFlow, PyTorch, Keras, and more are the tools that provide pre-built functions for your AI projects. The choice of libraries and frameworks depends on the specific requirements of your project.

d. *Integrated Development Environments (IDEs)*: Consider IDEs as the well-lit studio where you bring your AI visions to life. Jupyter Notebook, Visual Studio Code, and PyCharm are like comfortable artist studios, each offering a user-friendly interface for writing and running your AI code. Each IDE comes with unique features, and your selection may depend on your workflow and personal preference.

e. *Cloud-Based AI Services*: Think of cloud-based AI services as artist residencies, where you have access to a fully equipped studio. Cloud providers like AWS, Google Cloud, and Microsoft Azure offer pre-configured environments and powerful GPUs for your AI projects. They can be an excellent choice for those who want the flexibility of cloud-based solutions.

With the right hardware and software in place, you're equipped to embark on your AI journey. Just as an artist selects the right tools and materials for their masterpiece, you'll choose the components that best fit your AI projects, whether they involve image recognition, natural language processing, or any other creative AI endeavor. In the chapters ahead, you'll learn how to effectively use your chosen hardware and software to unlock the full potential of AI, regardless of your level of expertise.

Chapter 2: AI in the Workplace

Welcome to Chapter 2 of your AI journey, where we shift our focus from the foundation of AI to its practical applications in the professional landscape. In this chapter, we explore the exciting ways in which AI is reshaping the workplace. From project management and collaboration tools empowered by AI to virtual assistants streamlining work efficiency, AI-driven analytics aiding in informed decision-making, and the automation of repetitive tasks, we will delve into the transformative power of AI in the professional sphere.

In the following sections, we will uncover how AI is revolutionizing the management of projects and team collaborations. AI-driven tools are changing the game, making project workflows more efficient and team productivity soar. Get ready to witness the future of project management and collaboration.

As we delve deeper, meet your new virtual work companions, powered by AI. These digital assistants are not just voice-activated gadgets; they are essential allies in your pursuit of work efficiency. Discover how they can save you time, increase productivity, and make your workdays more manageable.

In the business world, data is a valuable asset. AI-driven analytics are the key to unlocking its potential. In this section, we'll explore how AI transforms raw data into actionable insights. See how AI empowers professionals to make informed decisions based on data-driven knowledge.

And finally, say goodbye to mundane, repetitive tasks. AI is here to streamline your workday by taking care of the routine. This section will show you how AI automation can free up your time, allowing you to focus on more strategic and creative aspects of your work. Get ready for a glimpse into a more efficient and productive professional life, courtesy of AI.

2.1. AI-Powered Project Management and Collaboration Tools

In the ever-evolving landscape of the modern workplace, the integration of artificial intelligence has brought forth a revolution in the way we manage projects and collaborate within teams. AI-powered tools have become indispensable companions, significantly enhancing productivity and efficiency. Let's explore AI-powered project management and collaboration tools and explore the profound impact they have on the professional world.

- **Asana** (https://asana.com): Asana, an AI-powered project management tool, is like having an experienced project manager at your side, offering insights and support in real-time. It leverages machine learning algorithms to analyze project data, predict potential roadblocks, and suggest optimal routes to project completion.

- **Trello** (https://trello.com): Trello's AI-infused project management tool revolutionizes project management by employing AI to provide insights into potential roadblocks and suggest the best paths for project completion. It's like having a virtual project manager guiding you through project complexities.

- **Slack** (https://slack.com)and **Microsoft Teams** (https://www.microsoft.com/en-us/microsoft-365/microsoft-teams/group-chat-software): These collaboration platforms utilize AI-driven chatbots to automate routine tasks, schedule meetings, and facilitate seamless communication. These digital assistants ensure that administrative tasks no longer impede your productivity, making team collaboration more efficient.

- **Monday.com** (https://monday.com) and **ClickUp** (https://clickup.com): These platforms use AI to automate repetitive project management tasks, such as setting deadlines, assigning tasks, and providing status updates. They free up your time and mental energy, allowing you to focus on the strategic aspects of your work.

- **Notion** (https://www.notion.so): Notion is a versatile workspace tool that integrates AI to adapt to your needs dynamically. It combines elements of project management and collaboration, offering a canvas for teams to design their workflows. Notion is increasingly popular among creative professionals and businesses.

- **Microsoft Cortana** (https://www.microsoft.com/en-us/cortana) and Google Assistant (https://assistant.google.com/): These virtual assistants offer AI-driven support for scheduling and note-taking, making daily tasks more manageable.

- **Tableau** (https://www.tableau.com/): Tableau is an AI-driven data analytics and visualization tool that transforms raw data into actionable insights for better decision-making.

- **Microsoft Azure** (https://azure.microsoft.com/): Microsoft Azure provides a wide array of AI services, including Azure Machine Learning, empowering professionals to harness the power of machine learning.

- **Microsoft Power BI** (https://powerbi.microsoft.com/): This business analytics tool comes with AI capabilities, enabling professionals to analyze data and make data-driven decisions.

- **Microsoft Dynamics 365** (https://dynamics.microsoft.com/en-us/): By integrating AI into CRM and ERP solutions, Microsoft Dynamics 365 AI enhances customer relationship management and enterprise resource planning.

- **Microsoft 365** (https://www.microsoft.com/en-us/microsoft-365/): Microsoft 365 includes AI-powered features for productivity and collaboration, offering a comprehensive suite of tools for professionals.

The introduction of AI into project management and collaboration tools isn't just about convenience; it's a fundamental shift in the way we work. These tools enable data-driven decision-making, enhance team communication, and liberate us from the monotony of repetitive tasks. As we delve into the details of these AI-powered solutions, you'll gain a deeper understanding of how they're reshaping the modern workplace and how you can leverage their capabilities to boost productivity and elevate collaborative efforts.

2.2. Virtual Assistants for Work Efficiency

In the digital age, virtual assistants have emerged as indispensable allies for enhancing

work efficiency and productivity. These AI-driven helpers are more than just novelties; they've become integrated into our daily professional routines, significantly streamlining tasks and improving the overall work experience. Let's explore how virtual assistants powered by AI are transforming the way we work and how you can harness their capabilities to achieve peak productivity.

- **Understanding Virtual Assistants**: Virtual assistants, powered by artificial intelligence, are designed to simulate human interactions. They come in various forms, including voice-activated assistants like Amazon's **Alexa** or Apple's **Siri** and text-based assistants like **Google Assistant**. These virtual helpers are versatile tools, offering practical solutions to simplify and optimize your daily tasks.

- **Scheduling and Calendar Management**: Virtual assistants excel at handling your busy schedule. For instance, you can simply instruct your virtual assistant to schedule a meeting with a colleague, and it will autonomously find suitable time slots based on your availability and that of your colleague. Microsoft's **Cortana** is renowned for its proficiency in this area, ensuring that your appointments and commitments are well-organized and conflict-free.

- **Note-Taking and Reminders**: One of the most valuable aspects of virtual assistants is their note-taking and reminder capabilities. Whether you have a brilliant idea during a brainstorming session or need to jot down a quick to-do list, virtual assistants can do it efficiently. They also send timely reminders for important tasks, ensuring that you stay on top of your work. **Google Assistant**, for example, can create notes, and shopping lists, and send you reminders for upcoming appointments, helping you manage your work seamlessly.

- **Voice Commands and Automation**: Voice-activated virtual assistants, like **Alexa**, have revolutionized the way we interact with our environments. They can control smart devices in your home or office, make calls, send texts, and perform web searches. If you're in the middle of a task and need information or a quick break, you can rely on your virtual assistant to answer your questions, play your favorite music, or even tell you a joke to lighten the mood.

- **Integration with Work Tools**: Many virtual assistants seamlessly integrate with popular work tools such as **Microsoft Office 365** and **G Suite**. This integration allows you to create and edit documents, send emails, and manage your work tasks without leaving the virtual assistant's environment. They serve as a bridge between your voice or text commands and your professional tools, making work tasks more convenient and efficient.

- **Multilingual Support**: In our increasingly globalized world, multilingual support is a crucial feature. Virtual assistants can help bridge language barriers, facilitating international business and collaboration. They can assist with translation tasks, making them essential for global teams working across different linguistic backgrounds.

By incorporating virtual assistants into your daily work routine, you can offload routine and time-consuming tasks, improve organization, and free up time for more complex and strategic work. Imagine having your virtual assistant schedule all your meetings, take notes during discussions, and send reminders for deadlines, all while you focus on creative problem-solving or strategic planning. This is the power of virtual assistants in enhancing work efficiency and productivity. In the sections to come, we'll delve deeper into these capabilities and explore the full potential of virtual assistants in the professional world.

2.3. AI-Driven Analytics for Informed Decision-Making

In today's data-driven world, making informed decisions is a fundamental aspect of success in any professional setting. AI-driven analytics has emerged as a game-changer in this regard, offering the ability to process vast datasets, identify trends, and provide actionable insights. In this section, we'll explore how AI-driven analytics empowers informed decision-making and provide examples to illustrate its impact.

The Role of AI in Data Analysis

AI-driven analytics leverages machine learning algorithms to process and analyze data at a scale and speed that surpasses human capabilities. It's not just about dealing with big data; it's about finding meaningful patterns, correlations, and insights within the data that can inform decision-making.

- ***Predictive Analytics***: AI-driven analytics can predict future trends and outcomes with impressive accuracy. For instance, e-commerce platforms like **Amazon** use AI to analyze past customer behavior and make product recommendations that increase sales. Similarly, financial institutions use predictive analytics to assess credit risk and detect fraudulent transactions.

- ***Customer Insights***: Understanding customer behavior is vital for businesses. AI-driven analytics tools like **Google Analytics** provide a wealth of data, allowing companies to identify which marketing strategies are working, which products are popular, and where customers are dropping off in the sales funnel.

- ***Healthcare Decision Support***: In healthcare, AI-driven analytics can analyze patient data to assist in diagnosis and treatment decisions. For example, **IBM Watson** analyzes patient records and medical literature to suggest personalized treatment options for cancer patients.

- ***Market Research:*** Companies use AI-driven analytics for market research.

They can analyze social media data, customer reviews, and surveys to gain insights into consumer sentiment and preferences. This informs product development, marketing strategies, and customer service improvements.

- *Operational Efficiency*: AI-driven analytics can optimize supply chains, manufacturing processes, and logistics. For example, companies like **Walmart** use AI to optimize their inventory management, ensuring that products are in stock when needed but not overstocked.

- *Risk Management*: In the financial industry, AI-driven analytics is used for risk assessment. Banks and insurance companies use AI to assess the risk associated with loans, investments, and insurance policies.

- *Natural Language Processing*: AI-driven analytics can process unstructured text data. Sentiment analysis tools like **Lexalytics** analyze social media conversations to gauge public opinion and sentiment about products, services, or political issues.

- *Churn Prediction*: Companies can use AI to predict customer churn. For instance,

Netflix analyzes user data to identify when a subscriber might cancel their subscription. This insight can inform retention strategies.

- *Recommendation Systems*: E-commerce and content platforms like **Netflix** and **Spotify** use AI-driven recommendation systems to suggest products or content to users based on their past behavior. These recommendations enhance user engagement and satisfaction.

By incorporating AI-driven analytics into your decision-making processes, you gain access to insights that were previously buried in massive datasets. These insights can inform strategic choices, help identify new opportunities, and mitigate risks. Whether you're in marketing, healthcare, finance, or any other industry, AI-driven analytics is a powerful tool for achieving informed decision-making. In the sections that follow, we'll dive deeper into specific applications and strategies for effectively using AI-driven analytics in the workplace.

2.4. Automating Repetitive Tasks with AI

One of the most immediate and transformative impacts of AI in the workplace is its ability to automate repetitive tasks. This not only saves time but also reduces the risk of errors,

freeing up professionals to focus on more strategic and creative aspects of their work. In this section, we'll explore how AI is automating repetitive tasks across various industries, providing real-world examples to illustrate the profound changes it's bringing about.

Understanding Task Automation:

AI-powered task automation involves the use of machine learning algorithms and robotic process automation (RPA) to take over routine, rule-based, and often time-consuming tasks. The AI systems can perform these tasks with accuracy and speed, reducing the burden on human workers.

- *Data Entry and Extraction*: AI-driven tools like **UiPath** and **Automation Anywhere** are extensively used in finance and data-centric industries to automate data entry and extraction tasks. For example, in a financial institution, AI can automatically extract relevant data from invoices, reducing the need for manual data entry.

- *Customer Support*: AI chatbots, such as **Zendesk's Answer Bot** and **Intercom's Resolution Bot**, can automate customer support by answering common queries, scheduling appointments, and guiding customers through basic troubleshooting. This not only improves customer satisfaction but also reduces the workload on support agents.

- *Content Generation*: Content creation, such as generating reports, articles, or product descriptions, is increasingly automated. **ChatGPT**, an AI language model, can generate human-like text. Companies like **OpenAI** are using AI to produce content for marketing and journalism.

- *Email Filtering and Sorting*: Inboxes can quickly become overwhelmed with emails. AI-powered tools like **SaneBox** can automatically filter and sort emails, categorizing them as important, spam, or newsletters. This reduces the time spent on email management.

- *Social Media Management*: Tools like **Hootsuite** and **Buffer** use AI to schedule and post content on social media platforms at optimal times, increasing engagement. They can also analyze the performance of social media campaigns.

- *Inventory and Supply Chain Management*: AI automates inventory management, ensuring that products are restocked when needed and minimizing excess inventory. **IBM Watson Supply Chain** is used for this purpose.

- *HR and Recruitment*: AI streamlines the hiring process by automating resume screening and even conducting initial interviews. **Workable** is an example of a platform that uses AI to help organizations find the right candidates more efficiently.

- *Data Analysis and Reporting*: In finance and business, AI automates data analysis and reporting. Tools like **Tableau** and **Power BI** can create interactive reports, reducing the time required for manual data analysis.

- *Security and Threat Detection*: AI-powered cybersecurity solutions like **Darktrace** use machine learning to identify and respond to potential threats in real time. This proactive approach enhances security by quickly detecting and mitigating risks.

- *E-commerce Personalization*: AI personalization engines, such as those used by **Amazon**, analyze user behavior and preferences to recommend products. This increases sales and improves the user experience.

- ***Telemedicine***: In healthcare, AI chatbots assist with patient intake and symptom assessment. **Babylon Health** is an example of a telemedicine platform that automates initial patient interactions.

Through the automation of these repetitive and time-intensive tasks, AI is not only elevating productivity but also mitigating the risk of human inaccuracies. This transformation is empowering professionals across diverse sectors, allowing them to refocus their energies on more valuable and strategic responsibilities, necessitating creative thought, rigorous analysis, and intricate issue-solving. Whether your domain is finance, customer support, content production, or any other field, grasping the utilization of AI for task automation can result in a significant shift in your daily work dynamics. In the forthcoming sections, we'll explore tactics for the efficient deployment of AI-driven automation.

Chapter 3: AI for Education

In the education field, the integration of artificial intelligence has brought about transformative changes that enhance the learning experience for students and educators alike. This chapter delves into the fascinating world of AI for education, exploring a range of innovative tools and platforms that are reshaping the way we acquire knowledge. We'll investigate AI tutors and personalized learning platforms that cater to individual needs, delve into tools for academic research and plagiarism detection, explore language learning aids and translation services, and immerse ourselves in the captivating realm of educational gaming and interactive content. The evolution of AI within the educational landscape promises to make learning more accessible, engaging, and effective, and in the sections to come, we'll uncover the exciting developments that are propelling education into the future.

3.1. AI Tutors and Personalized Learning Platforms

Education, once characterized by uniform curriculums and one-size-fits-all teaching, has undergone a revolutionary transformation with the introduction of AI tutors and personalized learning platforms. These technological innovations have opened doors to tailor-made educational experiences for students at all levels. In this section, we'll dive into the exciting world of AI tutors and personalized learning, exploring their applications, benefits, and real-world examples.

Personalized Learning: A Paradigm Shift

AI-driven personalized learning platforms have turned the traditional approach to education on its head. Rather than adhering to a rigid curriculum that progresses at a set pace, these platforms adapt to individual students' needs and learning styles. They do so by analyzing students' performance data and delivering content that matches their proficiency levels.

Benefits of AI Tutors and Personalized Learning:

- *Adaptive Learning*: AI tutors can adjust the difficulty of tasks in real time, ensuring students are appropriately challenged and engaged. For example, **DreamBox** in K-12 math education adapts math lessons to a student's performance.

- *Immediate Feedback*: AI tutors provide immediate feedback on assignments and quizzes, helping students understand their mistakes and make improvements. This accelerates the learning process.

- *Independence*: Personalized learning

platforms allow students to learn at their own pace. For instance, platforms like **Knewton** personalize college course materials, enabling students to advance when they are ready.

- ***Diversity of Content***: AI-driven platforms offer a variety of multimedia resources, catering to different learning styles. This fosters a more holistic approach to learning.

- ***Cost-Efficiency***: Personalized learning can be cost-effective, as it reduces the need for expensive printed materials and caters to a wide range of students.

Resources in the Field:

- ***DreamBox*** (https://www.dreambox.com/): This K-12 math platform employs AI to create individualized math lessons based on a student's progress and proficiency, making math engaging and comprehensible for students at various levels.

- ***Knewton*** (https://www.wiley.com/en-us/education/alta): Targeting higher education, Knewton personalizes college course materials to help students master the subject matter, taking into account their unique learning patterns and knowledge gaps.

- ***Carnegie Learning*** (https://www.carnegielearning.com/): This AI-driven platform delivers mathematics curriculums designed to adapt to each student's progress, making math education more approachable and effective.

- ***Coursera*** (https://www.coursera.org) and **edX** (https://www.edx.org): These are renowned online learning platforms that offer a wealth of educational courses from leading universities and institutions worldwide. Both platforms employ AI to provide personalized course recommendations, allowing learners to discover subjects aligned with their interests and career goals. Coursera offers a wide range of courses, degrees, and certificates, while edX provides a diverse array of high-quality courses and micro-degrees. These platforms have revolutionized online education, making learning accessible to anyone with an internet connection.

The integration of AI tutors and personalized learning platforms offers a dynamic, efficient, and effective way to educate students, catering to their unique needs and abilities, not only in K-12 but also in higher education. Whether in math education, writing, or any other field, these technologies have the potential to revolutionize how we learn, enabling students to reach their full potential and educators to provide tailored support. In the upcoming sections, we'll explore more facets of AI in education, uncovering the impact it has on academic research, language learning, and interactive content.

3.2. Tools for Academic Research and Plagiarism Detection

Academic research is the cornerstone of innovation and progress, and AI has not only accelerated the research process but has also played a vital role in upholding academic integrity through plagiarism detection tools. In this section, we delve into the impact of AI on academic research and explore the tools that aid researchers and educators in maintaining the highest standards of academic honesty.

AI in Academic Research

AI has revolutionized the landscape of academic research by streamlining data analysis, text mining, and knowledge discovery. Researchers can now process vast amounts of data and identify patterns and correlations that would be impossible to discern manually. For instance, the platform **IBM Watson** offers powerful AI tools for data analytics and knowledge extraction, making it an invaluable resource for researchers in various fields.

Plagiarism Detection

Maintaining academic integrity is of paramount importance, and AI-powered plagiarism detection tools have become indispensable in educational institutions. These tools compare students' work against a vast database of academic publications, websites, and other student submissions to identify instances of plagiarism. A well-known tool in this category is **Turnitin**, which provides comprehensive plagiarism checking for educational institutions worldwide.

Benefits of AI in Academic Research and Plagiarism Detection

- ***Efficient Data Analysis***: AI can rapidly analyze extensive datasets, identifying trends, correlations, and anomalies, enabling researchers to make data-driven decisions.

- ***Enhanced Knowledge Discovery***: AI tools can uncover valuable insights within academic literature, helping researchers identify gaps in existing knowledge and formulate new research questions.

- *Maintaining Academic Integrity*: Plagiarism detection tools like Turnitin act as a deterrent against academic dishonesty, ensuring fair evaluation of students' work.

- *Time Savings*: AI automates tasks such as literature review and data analysis, allowing researchers to focus on the more creative and analytical aspects of their work.

Resources in the Field

Here are some helpful AI-related resources for academic research and plagiarism detection:

- **IBM Watson** (https://www.ibm.com/watson): IBM Watson offers AI-powered tools for data analysis, natural language processing, and knowledge extraction, making it an asset for researchers across domains. Website

- **Turnitin** (https://www.turnitin.com): Turnitin is a widely used tool for plagiarism detection in educational institutions, ensuring academic integrity and honesty. Website

- **Grammarly** (https://www.grammarly.com): Grammarly is an

AI-driven writing assistant that helps researchers maintain proper grammar, spelling, and writing quality, which is crucial in academic writing.

- **Mendeley** (https://www.mendeley.com): While not a plagiarism detection tool, Mendeley is a reference manager that assists researchers in organizing and citing sources. It utilizes AI to recommend relevant research papers. Website

AI's influence on academic research and plagiarism detection is profound, offering researchers powerful tools to explore and analyze data. Moreover, it upholds academic integrity by providing educators with the means to ensure students' work is original and properly cited. In the following sections, we will further explore AI's role in language learning, translation, and interactive educational content.

3.3. Language Learning Aids and Translation

Language is the bridge that connects us to the world, and with the advent of AI, language learning and translation have become more accessible, efficient, and engaging. In this section, we'll explore how AI is transforming language education and bridging the gap between diverse cultures and languages through language learning aids and translation tools.

AI in Language Learning

Language learning has traditionally been a time-consuming and sometimes daunting task, requiring extensive memorization, practice, and often the assistance of a human tutor. AI has introduced a breath of fresh air into this field, making language acquisition more interactive and tailored to individual learners.

- *Personalized Learning*: AI-driven language learning platforms have the remarkable ability to adapt to the user's proficiency level. Whether you're a beginner or an advanced learner, platforms like **Duolingo** and **Rosetta Stone** offer customized lessons and practice exercises that match your skill level. This personalization ensures that you're consistently challenged and engaged in your language-learning journey.

- *Immediate Feedback*: One of the key challenges in language learning is getting feedback on pronunciation, grammar, and vocabulary usage. AI tutors within language learning apps offer real-time feedback, helping learners improve their language skills more effectively. This immediate feedback mechanism ensures that you're learning to speak and write accurately from the very beginning.

- *Gamification*: AI-powered language learning apps often incorporate gamified elements. This approach makes the learning process not only effective but also engaging and motivating. Platforms like **Duolingo** employ game-like challenges, rewards, and progress tracking to encourage regular practice and to make language learning feel like an enjoyable adventure.

- *Accessibility*: AI has made language learning more accessible by offering courses in numerous languages. Whether you want to explore languages from different regions or delve into languages that are not commonly taught in traditional classrooms, AI-driven platforms offer a wide range of choices, allowing learners to explore languages that pique their interest.

AI in Translation:

AI-powered translation tools have transcended traditional language barriers, enabling real-time communication and information sharing across the globe. Key aspects of AI-driven translation include:

- *Machine Translation*: AI algorithms used by tools such as **Google Translate** and **DeepL** analyze and translate text from one language to another. They provide instant and often accurate translations, making it easier for individuals to communicate and understand content in different languages.

- *Voice Translation*: AI enables real-time voice translation. Applications like **Microsoft Translator** and **iTranslate** facilitate spoken communication between individuals who speak different languages. This technology is particularly valuable for travelers, international business, and global communication.

- *Document Translation*: AI-powered platforms like **Lingviny** offer document translation services. They help businesses and individuals translate documents, contracts, and other written materials with ease, saving time and ensuring accurate translation.

Benefits of AI in Language Learning and Translation:

- *Efficiency*: AI accelerates the language

learning process, allowing learners to acquire new languages more rapidly. This efficiency is particularly beneficial for individuals who need to learn a language quickly for work, travel, or academic purposes.

- *Accessibility*: Language learning apps and translation tools break down linguistic barriers, promoting multicultural understanding and global communication. This accessibility fosters connections between individuals from diverse linguistic backgrounds.

- *Accuracy*: AI-driven translation tools offer increasingly accurate translations, minimizing language-related misunderstandings in both personal and professional contexts. Accurate translation is essential for business communication, international collaboration, and academic research.

- *Convenience*: AI empowers individuals to communicate and translate in real time. This convenience makes international travel and business more accessible, as well as allowing people to explore and appreciate content in different languages.

Resouces in the Field:

- ***Duolingo*** (https://www.duolingo.com) : A popular language learning platform that employs AI to offer personalized language courses, making learning languages engaging and accessible.

- ***Rosetta Stone*** (https://www.rosettastone.com): Known for its language learning software, Rosetta Stone uses AI to provide adaptive and immersive language learning experiences.

- ***Google Translate*** (https://translate.google.com): Google's AI-driven translation tool that can translate text, speech, and images, providing multilingual communication in real-time.

- ***DeepL*** (https://www.deepl.com/translator): A neural machine translation service known for its high-quality translations and language support.

- ***Microsoft Translator*** (https://www.microsoft.com/en-us/translator) : Offering voice translation and text translation, Microsoft Translator is a versatile tool for breaking language barriers.

AI's influence on language learning and translation is profound, enabling learners to master new languages more efficiently and promoting effective communication across linguistic divides. In the upcoming sections, we will explore AI's role in educational gaming and interactive content, highlighting how it's transforming the way we learn and engage with educational material.

3.4. Educational Gaming and Interactive Content

Education is evolving, and AI-driven educational gaming and interactive content are at the forefront of this transformation. In this section, we'll explore how AI is reshaping the learning experience, making it engaging, effective, and personalized through educational games and interactive content.

AI in Educational Gaming

Educational games have long been used to make learning more engaging for students, but AI has elevated these games to new heights. Here's how AI is impacting educational gaming:

- ***Personalized Learning Path***: AI algorithms within educational games analyze each student's performance and learning style. This data is then used to personalize the learning path, ensuring that students receive the content and challenges best suited to their individual needs. For example, the platform **Kahoot!** uses AI to adapt quizzes to students' proficiency levels and learning speeds.

- *Gamification for Engagement*: AI has introduced gamified elements into educational content, making learning more fun and motivating for students. Platforms like **Prodigy** use AI to create math games that adapt to students' progress, offering an enjoyable and educational experience.

- *Feedback and Progress Tracking*: AI-driven educational games provide instant feedback and detailed progress tracking. Students receive information on their strengths and weaknesses, allowing them to focus on areas that require improvement. **Minecraft: Education Edition**, for instance, tracks students' in-game activities and provides insights for teachers.

AI in Interactive Content

Interactive content, including simulations, virtual labs, and multimedia resources, benefits from AI in several ways:

- *Realistic Simulations*: AI enables the

creation of realistic simulations for educational purposes. For example, medical students can use AI-driven simulations for surgical training, while geography students can explore virtual landscapes to understand geographical concepts better.

- ***Personalized Learning***: Interactive content, powered by AI, can adapt to each student's pace and learning style. It can adjust difficulty levels, provide hints or explanations, and offer additional resources to enhance the learning experience. The platform **Smart Sparrow** provides adaptive elearning, tailoring content to individual learners.

- ***Language Learning Through Immersion***: AI-driven interactive language learning platforms like **Babbel** use immersive scenarios to help students learn languages. Through AI, learners are immersed in conversations and situations that mirror real-life language use.

Benefits of AI in Educational Gaming and Interactive Content:

- ***Engagement:*** Educational games and interactive content captivate students' interest, making learning more engaging and enjoyable.

- ***Personalization***: AI tailors the learning experience to each student, ensuring that they receive content and challenges that match their proficiency levels and learning styles.

- ***Feedback and Progress Tracking***: AI offers real-time feedback and tracks student progress, helping educators identify areas that need improvement and intervene when necessary.

- ***Hands-On Learning***: Interactive content, including simulations and virtual labs, enables students to gain practical experience and explore complex concepts in a safe environment.

Resources in the Field:

- ***Kahoot!***: An educational game-based platform that uses AI to adapt quizzes and challenges to individual students. Website: https://kahoot.com

- ***Prodigy***: A math game for students that employs AI to create adaptive challenges and motivate learning. Website: https://www.prodigygame.com

- ***Minecraft: Education Edition***: Utilizes AI to track students' in-game activities and provides insights for teachers. Website: https://education.minecraft.net

- ***Smart Sparrow***: Offers adaptive e-learning solutions through AI, personalizing content for students. Website: https://www.smartsparrow.com

- ***Babbel****:* An AI-driven language learning platform that uses immersive scenarios to teach languages effectively. Website: https://www.babbel.com

AI is transforming education by making learning more personalized, engaging, and interactive. Educational gaming and interactive content leverage AI to create an educational experience that suits each student's needs and learning style. In the upcoming sections, we'll explore AI's applications in healthcare, finance, and other fields, demonstrating its impact on various aspects of our lives.

Chapter 4: AI in Healthcare

The integration of AI in the healthcare sector marks a significant leap in the evolution of medical science and patient care. In this chapter, we delve into the remarkable ways in which AI is transforming the landscape of healthcare. From telemedicine and AI-assisted diagnosis to drug discovery and genomics, predictive analytics for patient outcomes, and the advent of remote monitoring and wearable AI devices, these advancements hold the potential to revolutionize healthcare as we know it.

AI is no longer a concept of the future but a present reality, reshaping the way we approach healthcare, enhancing medical research, and ultimately improving the lives of patients. This chapter explores the innovative AI applications that are saving lives, enhancing medical research, and bringing healthcare closer to people, irrespective of geographical boundaries. Join us on this journey through the intersection of artificial intelligence and medicine, where science fiction is now science fact.

4.1. Telemedicine and AI-Assisted Diagnosis

Telemedicine, empowered by AI-assisted diagnosis, is redefining healthcare accessibility and efficiency. This section explores the fusion of technology and medicine, showcasing how AI is shaping remote healthcare and transforming the

diagnostic process.

Telemedicine and Its Impact

Telemedicine is the provision of medical services and consultations remotely, often through video calls or other digital means. AI plays a pivotal role in telemedicine by enhancing the diagnostic capabilities of healthcare providers. Here's how it works:

- *Virtual Consultations*: With telemedicine, patients can consult with healthcare professionals without physically visiting a clinic or hospital. AI-powered platforms, like **Teladoc** and **Amwell**, facilitate these virtual appointments, allowing patients to seek medical advice from the comfort of their homes.

- *AI-Assisted Diagnosis*: During these virtual consultations, AI algorithms aid healthcare professionals in diagnosing medical conditions. For example, AI can analyze medical images, such as X-rays or MRIs, and provide immediate insights. **Zebra Medical Vision**, for instance, offers AI-driven diagnostic support for radiologists, helping them detect diseases in medical images more accurately.

- ***Accessibility***: Telemedicine bridges the geographical gap between patients and healthcare providers. It is particularly beneficial for individuals in remote or underserved areas who may not have easy access to healthcare facilities.

AI's Role in Diagnosis

AI-assisted diagnosis is a game-changer in healthcare. AI algorithms can process vast amounts of patient data, medical literature, and diagnostic images within seconds, resulting in quicker and more accurate diagnoses. This technology is particularly advantageous in the following ways:

- ***Faster Diagnosis***: AI can expedite the diagnosis process by rapidly analyzing patient data and offering preliminary assessments, which can be especially critical in emergency situations.

- ***Reduced Human Error***: AI-assisted diagnosis minimizes the potential for human error. It can detect subtle patterns or anomalies in medical images that might be missed by the human eye.

- ***Data-Driven Insights***: AI-driven systems leverage extensive datasets to provide insights and recommendations, contributing to more informed and evidence-based diagnoses.

Resources in the Field:

- **Teladoc** (https://www.teladoc.com): A telemedicine platform that offers virtual consultations with healthcare professionals. AI assists in diagnosing various medical conditions during these virtual visits.

- **Amwell** (https://business.amwell.com): Another telemedicine platform that provides virtual consultations, leveraging AI for diagnostic support.

- **Zebra Medical Vision** (https://zebramedical.com): A company that specializes in AI-driven diagnostic support for radiologists, enhancing their ability to detect diseases in medical images.

AI-assisted diagnosis in telemedicine is a testament to the synergy between technology and medicine. It not only improves healthcare accessibility but also enhances the accuracy and speed of diagnosis, ultimately benefiting patients and healthcare providers alike. In the following sections, we'll delve into AI's contributions to drug discovery and genomics, predictive analytics for patient outcomes, and the rise of remote monitoring through wearable AI devices in the healthcare sector.

4.2. Drug Discovery and Genomics

AI is revolutionizing drug discovery and genomics, ushering in an era of accelerated research, cost-effective drug development, and personalized medicine. In this section, we'll explore how AI is reshaping these critical aspects of healthcare.

AI-Powered Drug Discovery

Traditional drug discovery is a lengthy and costly process, but AI has injected new life into it by significantly speeding up the identification of potential drug candidates. Here's how AI is driving this transformation:

- *Virtual Screening*: AI algorithms can swiftly analyze vast databases of chemical compounds to identify potential drug candidates. **Atomwise**, for instance, employs AI for virtual drug screening, allowing researchers to predict how well a particular compound can interact with a specific target.

- *Predictive Models*: AI creates predictive models that help researchers anticipate a drug's behavior in the human body. These models not only expedite the development process but also increase the chances of success.

- ***Drug Repurposing***: AI can identify existing drugs that may be repurposed for new uses. For instance, AI has played a role in identifying potential treatments for conditions like COVID-19 by repurposing existing drugs.

Genomics and Precision Medicine

AI's influence extends to genomics, a field that explores an individual's genetic makeup. Here's how AI is making genomics more insightful:

- ***Personalized Medicine***: AI can analyze a patient's genetic data to tailor treatment plans. **23andMe** offers genetic testing and personalized health insights, enabling individuals to make informed decisions about their well-being based on their genetic information.

- ***Genome Sequencing***: AI facilitates rapid and cost-effective genome sequencing. Companies like **Illumina** use AI to process large volumes of genomic data efficiently.

- ***Disease Prediction***: AI models can predict

disease risks by analyzing genetic data. These insights are invaluable for preventive healthcare. For example, Color Genomics uses AI to assess genetic risks for conditions like cancer and heart disease.

Benefits of AI in Drug Discovery and Genomics:

- *Speed and Efficiency*: AI accelerates drug discovery and genomics research, saving time and resources.

- *Cost Reduction*: The use of AI in drug discovery reduces the cost of developing new drugs, making healthcare more affordable.

- *Precision Medicine*: AI enables personalized treatment plans, ensuring that patients receive therapies that suit their genetic makeup.

- *Disease Prevention*: AI helps identify disease risks early, enabling preventive healthcare measures.

Resources in the Field:

- *Atomwise* (https://www.atomwise.com): Utilizes AI for virtual drug screening, streamlining the process of identifying potential drug candidates. Website

- ***23andMe*** (https://www.23andme.com): Offers genetic testing and personalized health insights to individuals, empowering them to make informed health decisions. Website

- ***Illumina*** (https://www.illumina.com) : A company that employs AI for genome sequencing, providing insights into genetic data. Website

- ***Color Genomics*** (https://www.color.com): Uses AI for assessing genetic risks and disease prediction, with a focus on conditions like cancer and heart disease. Website

AI's impact on drug discovery and genomics is profound, offering solutions that are more precise, rapid, and cost-effective. This transformative technology is not only accelerating medical research but also ushering in an era of personalized medicine and preventive healthcare. In the upcoming sections, we'll explore AI's contributions to predictive analytics for patient outcomes and the rise of remote monitoring through wearable AI devices in healthcare.

4.3. Predictive Analytics for Patient Outcomes

Predictive analytics is reshaping the healthcare landscape by harnessing the power

 of AI to foresee patient outcomes. This section delves into how AI-driven predictive analytics is revolutionizing patient care and enabling healthcare providers to make informed decisions with far-reaching implications.

The Role of Predictive Analytics

Predictive analytics leverages AI to process vast datasets, clinical records, and patient information to anticipate outcomes. Here's how it's making an impact:

- *Early Detection*: Predictive analytics algorithms can identify high-risk patients and diseases in their early stages. For example, the **Johns Hopkins Hospital** uses predictive analytics to detect patient deterioration early, allowing healthcare providers to take preventive measures.

- *Treatment Personalization*: AI can assist in customizing treatment plans. It analyzes patient data to tailor therapies, medications, and interventions. **Cleveland Clinic** utilizes predictive analytics to personalize care, enhancing patient outcomes.

- *Resource Allocation*: Predictive analytics optimizes resource allocation by predicting patient admission rates and identifying areas of high demand. This helps hospitals allocate staff and resources efficiently.

Benefits of Predictive Analytics:

- *Enhanced Patient Outcomes*: Predictive analytics contributes to more favorable patient outcomes by allowing for early interventions and personalized care.

- *Resource Efficiency*: Hospitals and healthcare facilities can optimize their resources, reducing costs while maintaining high-quality care.

- *Improved Clinical Decision-Making*: Predictive analytics provides healthcare providers with actionable insights, enabling them to make informed decisions.

Examples in the Field:

- *Johns Hopkins Hospital*: Utilizes predictive analytics to detect patient deterioration early, enabling timely preventive measures.

- *Cleveland Clinic* (https://

my.clevelandclinic.org) and *Mayo Clinic* (https://www.mayoclinic.org): Use predictive analytics to personalize treatment plans, leading to improved patient outcomes.

Predictive analytics is a groundbreaking advancement in healthcare that transforms how patient outcomes are predicted and managed. By harnessing AI's capabilities, healthcare providers can detect issues early, offer personalized care, and allocate resources effectively, ultimately leading to better patient experiences and outcomes. Our journey through this chapter continues with a look at remote monitoring through wearable AI devices in healthcare.

4.4. Remote Monitoring and Wearable AI Devices

The integration of AI with remote monitoring and wearable devices has revolutionized healthcare by bringing proactive, personalized, and continuous health management within reach. In this section, we'll delve into how these technologies work and provide real-world examples to illustrate their significance.

The Role of Remote Monitoring and Wearable AI

Devices

Remote monitoring, often made possible through wearable AI devices, plays a pivotal role in modern healthcare:

- ***Continuous Health Tracking***: Wearable devices like the **Apple Watch** and **Fitbit** have evolved far beyond step counting. They now monitor a wide range of health metrics, from heart rate and sleep patterns to physical activity. This continuous, real-time monitoring empowers individuals to gain deeper insights into their well-being.

- ***Chronic Disease Management***: Patients with chronic conditions such as diabetes benefit greatly from wearable AI devices. For example, **Medtronic's Guardian Connect** system tracks glucose levels around the clock. This data not only helps individuals make informed decisions about their diet and insulin intake but also provides healthcare professionals with a comprehensive view of the patient's health.

- ***Post-Operative Care***: After surgery, patients often require close monitoring to ensure a smooth recovery. The **Tempus Pro** platform is a prime example of technology that enables healthcare providers to remotely monitor patients' vital signs and adjust treatment plans as needed.

- *Elderly Care*: Elderly individuals, especially those living independently, can rely on wearable AI devices for safety and well-being. **Philips Lifeline**, for instance, offers solutions that include fall detection and immediate access to emergency services, providing peace of mind for both seniors and their families.

Benefits of Remote Monitoring and Wearable AI Devices:

The advantages of integrating AI with remote monitoring and wearables are substantial:

- *Early Intervention*: Continuous monitoring enables the early detection of health irregularities, allowing for timely intervention and potentially preventing the escalation of health issues.

- *Improved Chronic Disease Management*: Patients with chronic conditions can actively participate in their care by tracking relevant health data, leading to better management and quality of life.

- *Enhanced Post-Operative Care*: Post-surgery monitoring becomes more effective and convenient, benefiting both patients and healthcare providers. Patients can recover in the comfort of their homes while being closely monitored.

- ***Elderly Care and Independence***: Wearable AI devices provide peace of mind for elderly individuals and their families. These devices allow seniors to maintain their independence while having immediate access to assistance when needed.

Examples/Resources in the Field:

- ***Apple Watch*** (https://www.apple.com/watch): The Apple Watch series offers continuous health tracking, including features like heart rate monitoring and electrocardiogram (ECG) recording. It has become a valuable tool for those seeking to maintain a healthy lifestyle.

- ***Fitbit*** (https://www.fitbit.com/global/us/home): Fitbit offers a range of wearable devices that track physical activity, sleep patterns, and various health metrics. It empowers individuals to lead healthier lives by providing insights into their well-being.

- ***Medtronic's Guardian Connect*** (https://www.medtronicdiabetes.com): Designed for diabetes management, the Guardian Connect system provides continuous glucose monitoring. It assists individuals in making informed decisions about their health and lifestyle.

- ***Tempus Pro*** (https://www.tempus.com): The Tempus Pro platform facilitates remote monitoring of patients' vital signs, making post-operative care more efficient and personalized.

The integration of AI with remote monitoring and wearable devices in healthcare exemplifies a proactive, patient-centric approach that improves healthcare quality, fosters independence, and enhances overall well-being. As we journey through this chapter, we'll further explore AI's influence on healthcare, including AI-powered diagnostics and telemedicine.

Chapter 5: AI in Creativity

As we transition from the realm of healthcare and its AI-driven innovations, we find ourselves on the threshold of a captivating journey into the world of creativity. In this chapter, we will embark on an exploration of how AI's influence manifests as a powerful muse, transforming and revitalizing the realms of content generation, digital art, music composition, and the enchanting world of video and photography editing.

In this captivating adventure, AI emerges as a catalyst for creative expression, offering a partnership that transcends mere automation. Beyond streamlining tasks, AI is an inspiring collaborator that provides artists, designers, musicians, and content creators with a treasure trove of innovative tools and methods. This opens doors to uncharted territories of artistic expression, expanding the horizons of what's possible in the realm of creativity.

Whether you're a wordsmith seeking inspiration, a visual artist yearning to experiment with new mediums, a musician in pursuit of unprecedented sounds, or a content creator aiming to elevate your storytelling, AI beckons you to embark on an exhilarating journey of exploration. It's a world where technology and artistry intertwine, promising novel possibilities and boundless creativity. In the pages that follow, we'll uncover how AI is shaping the future of creativity, providing innovative pathways for artists, visionaries, and innovators.

5.1. AI-Powered Content Generation for Writers and Marketers

In the dynamic landscape of content creation, AI has emerged as a game-changer, redefining how writers and marketers craft compelling narratives. This section takes you on a journey into the heart of AI-powered content generation, unraveling its profound influence on industries where the art of words holds sway.

The Evolution of Content Creation with AI

The realm of AI-powered content generation has undergone a remarkable evolution, moving beyond mere automation to become an indispensable tool for writers, marketers, and businesses alike. It draws upon natural language processing and machine learning to craft written content that closely emulates human communication.

Writers and marketers can leverage AI in several ways:

- ***Automating Content Production***: AI-powered platforms like **OpenAI's ChatGPT-3** and ChatGPT-4 have the capacity to churn out high-quality articles, blog posts, and marketing materials at a rapid pace. These AI systems analyze the input provided to them and generate contextually relevant content, saving writers valuable time and effort.

- ***Enhancing Creativity***: AI can serve as an inspirational partner by generating ideas, suggesting creative angles, and providing fresh perspectives. For instance, **CopyAI** assists in brainstorming ideas for various content types, helping writers overcome creative blocks.

- ***Improving SEO***: AI-driven tools like **MarketMuse** offer content optimization by analyzing search intent and competition. They provide recommendations to enhance content quality and ranking, a vital asset for marketers.

- ***Personalizing Marketing***: AI can tailor

content to specific audiences. Tools such as **Phrasee** specialize in generating personalized marketing copy, improving customer engagement and conversion rates.

Examples and Resources in the Field:

- ***OpenAI's ChatGPT-3*** (https://openai.com/chatgpt): This powerful AI language model generates human-like text based on input prompts. It's used in various content generation applications, like chatbots, content summarization, and more.

- ***CopyAI*** (https://www.copy.ai): An AI writing assistant that helps generate creative content ideas and drafts. It's a valuable resource for writers looking to overcome writer's block and brainstorm fresh content.

- ***MarketMuse*** (https://www.marketmuse.com): This AI platform analyzes your content against top-ranking pages, identifies gaps, and provides data-driven suggestions for improving content quality and SEO ranking.

- ***Phrasee*** (https://phrasee.co): Specializes in generating personalized marketing copy that resonates with target audiences. It optimizes email subject lines, social media posts, and ad copy to boost engagement and conversions.

AI's foray into content creation empowers writers and marketers with tools that not only streamline their work but also enhance creativity, audience engagement, and search engine visibility. As we navigate through this chapter, you'll witness how AI extends its transformative touch to various creative domains, including digital art, music composition, and the editing of videos and photographs.

5.2. Digital Art and Design Tools

The last section has unveiled the remarkable capabilities of AI in shaping the way we create written and marketing content. Now, as we step further into the realm of digital art and design, we'll discover how AI acts as a visionary collaborator in the world of visual expression. This section delves into a captivating domain where AI leverages its power to inspire and facilitate artistic innovation, redefining the landscape of digital art and design tools.

AI's Influence on Digital Art and Design:

AI has redefined the creative process in the field of digital art and design by introducing tools that facilitate, inspire, and expand artistic horizons. Here's how AI has made its mark:

- *Generative Art*: AI algorithms can generate intricate patterns, images, and designs. For instance, **Adobe Firefly** is an AI-powered tool that explores generative art, creating unique visual experiences. This tool allows artists to experiment with generative art, producing captivating visuals that are often impossible to create by hand.

- *Immersive Art*: Platforms like **MidJourney** employ AI to create immersive and interactive artistic experiences, merging technology and art to offer captivating narratives. These immersive experiences transport viewers to fantastical worlds, blurring the lines between reality and art.

- *Photo Enhancement*: AI enhances photo editing with tools such as **Topaz Labs**, offering features like AI upscaling, noise reduction, and creative filters. These tools empower photographers and graphic designers to achieve professional-quality results with minimal effort.

- *Color Harmony*: **Khroma** utilizes AI

to help designers and artists discover harmonious color palettes and generate color schemes. This assists creators in achieving visually pleasing and cohesive designs.

- *Visual Storytelling*: **DreamStudio** is an AI-driven platform that assists in the creation of visual narratives and storytelling through automated image generation. This tool simplifies the process of visual storytelling, making it accessible to a broader audience.

- *Sketch Assistance*: Tools like **AutoDraw** use AI to recognize doodles and sketches, turning them into more refined and recognizable images. This feature aids individuals in transforming rough sketches into polished illustrations, making drawing more approachable.

- *Logo Design*: **Looka Logo Maker** leverages AI to generate logos tailored to a brand's identity, simplifying the logo design process. Small businesses and entrepreneurs can now create professional logos without the need for extensive design skills.

- *Prototyping*: **Uizard** is an AI-powered tool that transforms sketches into interactive prototypes for web and app design. This streamlines the prototyping phase of web and app development, saving time and resources.

- *Graphic Design*: **Canva** integrates AI to provide design suggestions, templates, and creative assistance for a wide range of projects. This makes graphic design accessible to individuals with varying levels of design expertise, from beginners to professionals.

Examples and Resources in the Field:

- *Adobe Firefly* (https://www.adobe.com/sensei/generative-ai/firefly.html): Adobe's AI-powered tool for generative art, offering a canvas for creative exploration. Artists can use this tool to experiment with generative art, producing captivating visuals.

- *MidJourney* (https://www.midjourney.com): An artistic platform merging AI and immersive experiences, creating interactive narratives. Viewers can immerse themselves in fantastical worlds, blurring the lines between art and reality.

- *Topaz Labs* (https://www.topazlabs.com): An AI-driven photo editing tool, enhancing images and enabling creative filters. This tool empowers photographers and graphic designers to achieve professional-quality results.

- **Khroma** (https://www.khroma.co): A tool for discovering color harmony and generating color palettes with AI assistance. Designers and artists can create visually pleasing and cohesive designs.

- **DreamStudio** (https://dreamstudio.com/about): An AI platform for visual storytelling and automated image generation. This simplifies visual storytelling, making it accessible to a broader audience.

- **AutoDraw** (https://www.autodraw.com): A sketch recognition tool using AI to refine doodles into recognizable images. This feature aids individuals in transforming rough sketches into polished illustrations.

- **Looka Logo Maker** (https://looka.com): AI-powered logo design for branding and visual identity. Small businesses and entrepreneurs can create professional logos.

- **Uizard** (https://uizard.io): Transform

sketches into interactive prototypes for web and app design with AI. This streamlines the prototyping phase of web and app development.

- ***Canva*** (https://www.canva.com): An AI-integrated graphic design platform, offering design suggestions and creative assistance. This makes graphic design accessible to individuals with varying levels of design expertise.

- ***Microsoft Designer*** (https://designer.microsoft.com): Microsoft's AI platform offers innovative design tools and templates for various applications.

- ***Microsoft Bing Image Creator*** (https://www.bing.com/create): An AI-powered platform for image creation, simplifying the process of generating visuals and artwork.

AI's involvement in the realm of digital art and design isn't just about automation; it's more like AI and artists joining forces to supercharge creativity. Whether you're a digital artist, a graphic designer, or simply someone who loves art, AI brings a cool toolbox to help you explore and take your creativity to new heights. As you read through this chapter, you'll see how AI is shaking up creativity in exciting ways, from making music to sprucing up your videos and photos.

5.3. Music Composition and Production with AI

As we delve deeper into the realm of AI's creative influence, we transition from the visual arts to the harmonious world of music composition and production. In this section, we explore how AI has orchestrated transformative changes in the music industry, offering novel ways for musicians, composers, and music enthusiasts to craft melodies and harmonies. Let's embark on this musical journey, discovering resources and platforms that harmoniously blend AI's ingenuity with human creativity.

Evolution of AI in Music

AI has introduced a dynamic shift in music composition and production, bridging technology with artistry:

- **Soundraw.io** provides an accessible platform for creating music, driven by AI-generated chord progressions. Musicians of all levels can leverage AI's musical insights to craft captivating melodies, exploring a harmonious partnership between human creativity and technology. Visit the website here: https://soundraw.io

- **AIVA (Artificial Intelligence Virtual Artist)** represents a harmonious blend of human direction and AI's extensive musical knowledge, enabling users to compose original music compositions. It embodies the evolution of AI in music as a collaborative partner in the creative process. See more details about AIVA via this website: https://www.aiva.ai

- **Amper Music** offers a versatile tool that employs AI to compose music for various purposes, from film scoring to content creation. It exemplifies AI's role in music, serving as a valuable resource for musicians seeking creative assistance from technology. Visit website here: https://ampermusic.zendesk.com/hc/en-us

- **Google Magenta** showcases the cutting-edge research and developments in AI's contribution to the creative arts. Musicians and artists can explore a multitude of tools and models to craft AI-generated compositions, reflecting the ongoing transformation of music creation. Explore more information here:

https://magenta.tensorflow.org

- ***Soundful*** takes a collaborative approach to music creation, where users provide their musical preferences, and AI contributes to crafting personalized melodies. This approach highlights the evolving trend of AI-powered music that respects individuality and artistic expression. Soundful website: https://soundful.com

- ***Boomy*** simplifies the music creation process with AI, allowing users to compose, produce, and share music with ease. This represents the evolving trend of democratizing music creation, making it accessible to a broader audience through AI. Visit Boomy here: https://boomy.com

AI in Music Today

The landscape of AI in music composition and production is continuously evolving, reflecting a shift from traditional methods to innovative AI-powered solutions. Today, musicians and composers find themselves at a unique intersection of human artistry and technological innovation, where AI serves as a creative partner rather than a replacement for human talent. These real-world platforms and resources, driven by AI, represent the ongoing transformation of music creation and production, opening new creative horizons and enriching the musical journey.

AI's presence in music composition and production harmonizes with human creativity, introducing innovative methods and expanding artistic horizons. Whether you're a seasoned composer or an aspiring musician, these AI-powered tools offer a symphony of creative possibilities. As we progress through this chapter, you'll witness AI's influence extending into other domains of creativity, from video and photograph editing to uncharted artistic horizons, inspiring your own creative journey.

5.4. AI-Enhanced Video and Photography Editing

AI's creative influence extends to video and photography editing, revolutionizing these visual mediums. It provides artists, photographers, and videographers with tools and resources that streamline editing processes and elevate creativity. Let's delve into AI's impact on enhancing video and photography editing, complete with practical examples and resources for your visual storytelling journey.

AI in Video Editing

AI-powered video editing tools have simplified the process of creating professional-level videos. Whether you're a content creator, filmmaker, or just someone who enjoys recording and sharing videos, these AI tools can help you achieve stunning results:

- ***Lumen5***: Lumen5 is an AI-driven video creation platform that transforms text content into engaging video presentations. It's a valuable resource for content creators looking to breathe life into their written words. Learn more here: https://lumen5.com

- ***Magisto***: Magisto is an AI video editor that helps users create impressive videos without the need for extensive editing skills. With AI-powered features, it's a great solution for individuals and businesses looking to craft professional video content. Visit Magisto for more information: https://www.synthesia.io

- ***Wondershare Filmora***: Filmora is a user-friendly video editing software with AI features that simplify the editing process. It's suitable for both beginners and experienced video editors. See more information of Filmora: https://filmora.wondershare.com

- ***Descript***: Descript is an AI-driven transcription and video editing tool that allows users to edit videos by editing the transcribed text. It's a unique and efficient way to work on your video content. Explore Descript here: https://www.descript.com

- ***Vidyo.ai***: Vidyo.ai offers AI-powered video editing and enhancement tools, making it easier to improve the quality of your video content. Visit Vidyo.ai here: https://vidyo.ai

- ***Adobe Premiere Pro***: Adobe's flagship video editing software now incorporates AI features like Auto Reframe, which automates the process of resizing videos for different platforms. It streamlines the video editing process for professionals. Learn more here: https://www.adobe.com/products/premiere.html

AI in Photography Editing

AI has brought significant enhancements to photography editing, making it easier for both amateur and professional photographers to achieve stunning results. Here are some notable AI-powered resources:

- ***Adobe Photoshop***: Adobe Photoshop has integrated AI features like the "Enhance Details" tool, which uses machine learning to enhance image details while minimizing artifacts. This empowers photographers with advanced editing capabilities. Visit Adobe Photoshop here: https://www.adobe.com/products/photoshop.html

- ***PortraitPro***: PortraitPro utilizes AI to enhance portrait photography. It simplifies tasks like retouching and enhancing facial features, making it an excellent tool for portrait photographers. Learn more about PortraitPro: https://www.anthropics.com/portraitpro

- ***Luminar***: Luminar offers AI-driven photo editing capabilities, including AI Sky Replacement and AI Structure, which enhance images with ease. It's a valuable resource for photographers seeking creative editing tools. Visit Luminar here: https://skylum.com/luminar

AI-Enhanced Editing Today

The advent of AI in video and photography editing simplifies the creative process, whether you're editing your vacation photos or crafting a professional video for your business. These AI-powered tools offer a broad spectrum of creative possibilities, making visual storytelling more accessible than ever. As we delve deeper into this chapter, you'll witness AI's influence extending into other creative domains, inspiring you to explore new horizons in your artistic journey.

AI has become a creative ally, simplifying the editing of videos and photographs and opening new horizons for visual storytelling. Whether you're a content creator, filmmaker, photographer, or anyone with a passion for visual expression, these AI-powered resources offer a wealth of creative potential. In the upcoming sections, we'll explore AI's role in redefining creativity across various other domains, from content generation to digital artistry.

Chapter 6: AI in Entertainment and Leisure

As we journey from the creative realms of music, video, and photography editing, we now step into the exciting universe of entertainment and leisure, where AI's transformative influence knows no bounds. In this chapter, we will explore how AI becomes your ultimate companion in entertainment, making recommendations for movies, music, and books that match your preferences. We'll venture into the realm of virtual and augmented reality, where AI takes us on immersive adventures. Then, we'll dive into gaming, where AI generates thrilling content. Finally, we'll explore AI's role in sports analysis and coaching. Join us as we discover how AI redefines the art of leisure, transforming the way we unwind, experience, and play.

6.1. AI-Powered Recommendation Engines for Movies, Music, and Books

This section focuses on AI-powered recommendation engines for movies, music, and books. It sheds light on how artificial intelligence is revolutionizing content discovery, making it a more personalized and enjoyable experience. Whether you're passionate about films, music, or books, AI is your partner in enhancing content discovery. Let's dive into the mechanisms behind these recommendation engines and witness the transformation AI brings to our entertainment consumption.

Movie Recommendations

AI-powered services like **Netflix**, **Amazon Prime**, and **IMDb** use recommendation algorithms to suggest movies and TV shows based on your viewing history. For example, if you're a fan of science fiction, these platforms will analyze your past selections and propose films in the same genre. This AI-driven curation saves you time and introduces you to hidden cinematic gems.

Music Discovery

Spotify's recommendation system is a prime example of AI at work in the music domain. It examines your listening history and generates personalized playlists and music suggestions. If you often enjoy jazz, it will introduce you to new jazz artists or albums. This not only broadens your musical horizons but also keeps your playlists fresh and exciting.

Book Suggestions

Online booksellers like **Amazon** and **Goodreads** employ AI-driven book recommendation engines to help you discover new authors and genres. They analyze your book browsing history and purchase choices to propose novels that you might find captivating. These recommendations open doors to literary adventures you may not have encountered otherwise.

Examples and Resources in the Field:

- ***Netflix***: The streaming giant employs AI to recommend movies and TV shows based on your watching behavior. Visit website: https://www.netflix.com

- ***Spotify***: This music streaming platform's recommendation system offers personalized playlists like "Discover Weekly" to keep your ears delighted. Learn more here: https://open.spotify.com

- ***Amazon***: The online retail giant uses AI algorithms to suggest books and products based on your browsing and purchase history. Visit the website here: https://www.amazon.com

- ***Goodreads***: As a platform dedicated to readers, Goodreads uses AI to suggest books tailored to your preferences, helping you explore new literary worlds. Learn more here: https://www.goodreads.com

- ***YouTube***: The YouTube recommendation algorithm suggests videos based on your previous watches and searches, introducing you to content that aligns with your interests. Learn more here: https://www.youtube.com

- ***Pandora***: This music streaming service

uses the Music Genome Project, a music database driven by AI, to recommend songs based on their musical characteristics. Visit the website here: https://www.pandora.com

AI recommendation engines have become indispensable in guiding your entertainment choices. By understanding your unique preferences, they enhance your leisure time by connecting you with content that resonates with you. In the following sections, we'll delve into AI's influence in virtual and augmented reality experiences, gaming, and sports analysis, showing how it's transforming various facets of our entertainment and leisure activities.

6.2. Virtual Reality and Augmented Reality Experiences

Virtual reality (VR) and augmented reality (AR) have evolved significantly over the years, fundamentally transforming the way we engage with the digital realm and bridging the gap between reality and the virtual. These technologies immerse us in captivating and interactive experiences that reconfigure our perceptions of the digital world. At the heart of this transformation lies AI, which plays a pivotal role in enhancing these experiences by infusing them with a sense of realism and responsiveness that is nothing short of remarkable.

AI in Virtual Reality

Virtual reality simulates immersive environments that transport us to new worlds. AI heightens this immersion in various ways:

1. ***Immersive Gaming***: AI algorithms in VR games create dynamic and adaptable environments. For example, "Half-Life: Alyx" employs AI-driven enemies that respond intelligently to a player's actions, enhancing the thrill of combat. The enemies' behaviors evolve based on your tactics, making each encounter unique and engaging.

2. ***Training Simulations***: Industries use VR and AI to provide training scenarios. Flight simulators, for instance, replicate real-life flying experiences, aided by AI that responds realistically to a pilot's actions. This technology is particularly valuable in preparing professionals for high-stakes situations.

3. ***Therapeutic Applications***: VR, guided by AI, helps individuals confront their fears or phobias gradually. AI adapts the VR experience based on the user's comfort

level, making it an effective therapeutic tool for mental health professionals. By adjusting the level of exposure and content in real-time, it fosters a gradual and manageable therapeutic journey.

AI in Augmented Reality

Augmented reality overlays digital content onto the real world, enhancing our understanding and interactions. AI plays a critical role in these applications:

1. *Navigation*: AR apps like Google Maps use AI to display real-time directions and information on your screen as you navigate through a city. By recognizing your surroundings and providing context-sensitive data, these apps make navigation more intuitive and efficient.

2. *Visual Search*: Apps like Snapchat and Google Lens use AR and AI to recognize objects and provide information about them in real-time. This technology is expanding our understanding of the world by providing instant information about landmarks, plants, and more.

3. *Education and Training*: AR applications in education, such as AR anatomy apps, use AI to provide interactive learning experiences. By recognizing images in

textbooks or posters and overlaying 3D models or animations, students can gain a deeper understanding of complex subjects.

4. *Shopping*: AR apps enable users to try on virtual clothes, see how furniture fits in their homes, and even preview makeup looks. AI algorithms ensure that virtual items align seamlessly with the physical world, offering an interactive and convenient shopping experience.

Resources in the Field:

- *Half-Life: Alyx*: This VR game features AI-driven enemies that adapt to your gameplay style, adding an element of unpredictability and excitement. Learn more here: https://www.half-life.com/en/alyx

- *Microsoft HoloLens*: A leading AR headset that integrates AI for mixed reality experiences, bringing digital elements seamlessly into the real world. Visit Microsoft HoloLens here: https://www.microsoft.com/en-us/hololens

- *Google Maps*: The navigation app employs AR and AI to enhance your real-world navigation, helping you find your way with real-time information. Visit Google

Maps here: https://www.google.com/maps

- ***Snapchat***: This social media platform uses AR and AI for interactive filters and lenses, transforming your selfies and videos into playful and engaging experiences. Learn about Snapchat here: https://www.snapchat.com

- ***Zappar***: An AR platform that combines AI and AR for creative content delivery, empowering businesses and creators to craft immersive AR experiences. Learn about Zappar here: https://www.zappar.com

As we dive into the world of AI-enhanced VR and AR, we'll discover the ingenious ways these technologies are reshaping entertainment, education, and everyday experiences. Emerging from the domain of AI recommendation engines that refine our entertainment choices, we now step into the immersive landscapes of virtual and augmented reality, where AI takes our digital experiences to new heights, fostering engagement, learning, and interaction in ways previously unimaginable.

6.3. Gaming with AI-Generated Content

In the gaming universe, AI emerges as a creative force reshaping the very fabric of

digital entertainment. It does so by generating content that reacts to players, providing unique challenges, and building entire game worlds that are ever-evolving. This is a dynamic fusion of human ingenuity and AI's computational prowess, delivering a gaming experience that surpasses imagination.

- **Procedural Generation:** One of AI's revolutionary impacts is procedural generation. No Man's Sky, developed by Hello Games, employs AI to conjure an entire universe teeming with planets, vegetation, and wildlife. Each player embarks on a profoundly personal journey through this virtually boundless galaxy, as AI algorithms dynamically craft terrains, creatures, and weather patterns. The result? An endlessly diverse, captivating cosmos where no two planets are alike.

- **Adaptive Storytelling:** Games like "Detroit: Become Human," created by Quantic Dream, demonstrate how AI enhances adaptive storytelling. Here, the choices players make influence the narrative, giving rise to a multitude of potential storylines. AI meticulously tracks player decisions and adapts the plot accordingly, making each playthrough a unique and unforgettable experience.

- **AI-Powered NPCs:** Non-playable characters (NPCs) have become remarkably sophisticated and lifelike, thanks to AI. In the open-world epic "Red Dead Redemption 2" by Rockstar Games, NPCs display convincingly realistic behaviors influenced by their surroundings and interactions with players. They engage in activities like hunting, socializing, and dynamically reacting to the player's actions, crafting an immersive Wild West experience.

- **Game Modding:** AI also empowers players to be creators. Generative Adversarial Networks (GANs) have paved the way for tools like Artbreeder, granting users the ability to generate and customize game assets, characters, and even environments. AI-generated mods offer gamers limitless possibilities for tailoring their gaming experiences to their preferences.

Resources in the Field:

- ***No Man's Sky***: Explore a universe shaped by AI, where each planet is a unique, AI-crafted gem. Learn more here: https://www.nomanssky.com

- ***Detroit: Become Human***: Witness AI-driven storytelling at its finest, with narratives that adapt to your choices. Learn more here: https://www.quanticdream.com/en/detroit-become-human

- ***Red Dead Redemption 2***: Immerse yourself in a Wild West world teeming with AI-powered NPCs whose lives are shaped by their environment and your actions. Visit this link for more information: https://www.rockstargames.com/reddeadredemption2

- ***Artbreeder***: A platform powered by AI that lets gamers create and modify game assets, characters, and environments, offering a limitless canvas for creative customization. Lear more here: https://www.artbreeder.com

As we journey deeper into the boundless realms of AI-infused gaming, players find themselves in dynamically shifting worlds that adapt, react, and evolve in sync with their actions. This chapter will continue to explore AI's multifaceted role in entertainment and leisure, from the creation of immersive sports analysis tools to innovations poised to redefine our leisure activities.

6.4. AI in Sports Analysis and Coaching

In the world of sports, precision and strategy can mean the difference between victory and defeat. Artificial Intelligence has swiftly become an essential player, revolutionizing the way athletes train, compete, and win. AI's prowess extends from in-depth performance analysis to personalized coaching, making it an invaluable ally for sports enthusiasts at every level.

- **Performance Analytics:** AI-driven sports analytics systems, such as those from Second Spectrum, StatSports, and Catapult, have the ability to dissect every move on the field. They utilize complex algorithms to track player positions, movements, and vital statistics in real-time. Teams and athletes leverage this data to gain invaluable insights into their performance, discovering strengths and weaknesses to optimize their game strategies.

- **Computer Vision for Action Recognition:**

Computer vision-powered AI can recognize and interpret sports actions. For example, in basketball, an AI system can automatically detect a slam dunk, a three-point shot, or a block, allowing for deeper performance analysis and creating highlight reels with pinpoint accuracy.

- **Wearable Technology:** Wearable AI devices like WHOOP and Catapult's PLAYR have gained popularity among athletes. These tools track biometric data, including heart rate, sleep patterns, and activity levels. The data is analyzed to help athletes make critical decisions on recovery and training optimization, ultimately leading to enhanced on-field performance.

- **Personalized Coaching:** AI-driven coaching apps and platforms, like Hudl Technique and Blast Motion, provide personalized feedback to athletes. These systems use motion capture and AI algorithms to assess an athlete's form, technique, and physical condition, helping individuals refine their skills and reach their full potential.

Resources in the Field:

- *Second Spectrum*: A leader in AI-powered

sports analytics, providing teams and players with comprehensive performance insights. Visit the website here: https://www.secondspectrum.com/index.html

- **StatSports**: Utilizes AI to track and analyze athlete performance, providing data-driven solutions for improvement. Learn more here: https://statsports.com

- **Catapult**: A global technology provider for sports, known for wearable tech that monitors player metrics in real time. Visit the website here: https://www.catapult.com

- **WHOOP**: A wearable device focused on athlete recovery, sleep optimization, and performance improvement through AI analytics. Learn more here: https://www.whoop.com/us/en

- **Hudl Technique**: An AI-driven coaching platform that enables athletes to analyze their technique and receive personalized feedback. Visit the website here: https://www.hudl.com

- **Blast Motion**: Offers AI-enhanced motion capture for athletes, helping them refine their skills and achieve peak performance. Learn more here: https://blastmotion.com

AI in sports transcends the conventional understanding of training and performance. It introduces a new era of precision, providing athletes, coaches, and teams with unparalleled insights to excel on the field. As we explore further into this chapter, we'll witness AI's impact on various aspects of our leisure activities, from crafting personalized entertainment recommendations to redefining virtual and augmented reality experiences.

Chapter 7: AI for Personal Development

Moving from our exploration of AI in the realms of entertainment and leisure, we now venture into Chapter 7: "AI for Personal Development." This chapter discusses how AI becomes a valuable companion in the journey of personal growth and well-being. It aids us in achieving healthier lifestyles, increased mindfulness, and smarter financial decisions. AI acts as a catalyst for our self-improvement, demonstrating its transformative influence across diverse facets of our lives.

7.1. Personalized Fitness and Nutrition Recommendations

Fitness Recommendations

AI-powered fitness apps and wearables have revolutionized how we approach physical activity and exercise. They offer personalized guidance, real-time monitoring, and data-driven insights that help users stay motivated and maintain healthier lifestyles. T

ke, for instance, Fitbit, one of the most recognized names in the realm of fitness wearables. Fitbit tracks your daily activity levels, monitors your heart rate, and even analyzes your sleep patterns. Using this information, it provides tailored recommendations and goals to encourage you to lead an active life. The app's virtual coach celebrates your achievements and helps you overcome fitness plateaus, ensuring that your journey to better health remains engaging and rewarding.

Another remarkable AI-driven fitness tool is the Freeletics app, known for its adaptive and customized approach to exercise. Whether you're a novice taking your first steps on the path to fitness or a seasoned athlete looking for new challenges, Freeletics designs workout routines to suit your fitness level and personal goals. The AI-driven coaching provides real-time feedback, adjusting the intensity of your workouts to match your performance. The result is an exercise plan that evolves with you, preventing monotony and maximizing your fitness potential.

Nutrition Guidance

AI's role in personal development isn't limited to physical activity; it extends to the realm of nutrition. With the support of AI-driven apps, managing your diet and making informed nutritional choices has never been easier. Apps like MyFitnessPal have gained immense popularity for their comprehensive approach to nutrition. MyFitnessPal enables users to monitor their food intake, count calories, and assess the nutritional value of the foods they consume. The app's vast database contains a wide range of food items, making it easy to log your meals and snacks. It then leverages AI to offer insights into your dietary habits, helping you identify areas for improvement. By tailoring its recommendations to your health and fitness goals, it becomes a valuable companion on your journey towards better nutrition and well-being.

Nutrino, another outstanding AI-driven application, specializes in creating personalized meal plans. It takes into account your specific dietary requirements, such as allergies, restrictions, or preferences, and offers meal suggestions and recipes that align with your needs. Whether you're aiming to lose weight, build muscle, or simply eat more healthily, Nutrino ensures that your meals are not only nutritionally balanced but also appealing to your taste buds. This kind of personalized nutrition guidance ensures that you can stick to your dietary goals while savoring a variety of delicious, healthful dishes.

Resources in the Field:

- *Fitbit*: Fitbit is a leading fitness wearable that tracks your activity, monitors your vital signs, and provides personalized recommendations to help you stay on the path to wellness. Learn more here: https://www.fitbit.com/global/us/home

- *Freeletics*: Freeletics is an AI-powered fitness app that designs customized workouts based on your fitness level and goals, providing real-time feedback to optimize your performance. Visit the website here: https://www.freeletics.com/en

- *MyFitnessPal*: MyFitnessPal is a versatile nutrition app that assists you in monitoring your food consumption and delivers dietary insights. Learn more here:

https://www.myfitnesspal.com

- ***Nutrino***: Nutrino offers tailored meal plans and recipes to align with your nutritional needs and goals, making healthy eating more manageable and enjoyable. Visit the website here: https://www.nutrinohealth.com

AI's influence on fitness and nutrition isn't merely about tracking; it acts as a virtual fitness trainer and nutritionist, collaborating with you to help achieve your health and wellness objectives. As we progress through this chapter, we'll uncover how AI contributes to mental well-being, language learning, and financial management, fostering holistic personal development.

7.2. Mindfulness and Mental Health Applications

In our fast-paced, digitally connected world, stress, anxiety, and other mental health concerns have become prevalent. This is where AI steps in, offering a range of mindfulness and mental health applications that can help individuals better manage their emotional well-being.

1. **Headspace** (https://www.headspace.com): Headspace is a popular mindfulness app that employs AI to deliver personalized meditation sessions, promoting relaxation and emotional balance. The app offers guided meditation sessions, and techniques to reduce stress, improve focus, and enhance overall mental health. It adapts to your needs, helping you build a consistent mindfulness practice that can lead to increased relaxation and emotional balance.

2. **Woebot** (https://woebothealth.com): For individuals struggling with conditions like anxiety, depression, or insomnia, Woebot serves as a digital mental health coach. This AI-driven chatbot offers therapeutic conversations and cognitive-behavioral techniques, which are evidence-based methods for managing these conditions. Woebot engages users in daily conversations, helping them identify negative thought patterns, develop healthier habits, and cope with

their emotional challenges.

3. **Calm** (https://www.calm.com): Calm is another popular mindfulness app that employs AI for enhancing mental well-being. It offers guided meditation sessions, sleep stories, and relaxation exercises. Calm's AI algorithms suggest content tailored to your needs, whether you want to reduce stress, improve your sleep, or simply relax.

4. **Talkspace** (https://www.talkspace.com): Talkspace is an online therapy platform that connects users with licensed therapists. While not an AI in the traditional sense, it leverages technology to improve access to mental health services. Users can communicate with therapists through text, audio, or video, making therapy more convenient and accessible.

5. **Youper** (https://www.youper.ai): Youper is an AI chatbot designed to assist users in tracking their mood, offering emotional support, and using evidence-based therapeutic techniques. It's particularly helpful for those dealing with mood disorders and emotional regulation.

6. **BetterHelp** (https://

www.betterhelp.com): BetterHelp is an online counseling platform that connects individuals with licensed therapists. It employs AI to match users with therapists based on their needs and preferences, making the process of finding professional help more efficient.

These AI-driven mindfulness and mental health apps play a crucial role in assisting individuals in navigating their emotional well-being. They provide accessible and cost-effective support, reducing the stigma associated with seeking help for mental health issues. As we delve deeper into this chapter, we'll explore AI's role in language learning and personal finance, two additional domains that are vital for holistic personal development.

7.3. AI-Driven Personal Finance and Investment Advice

Managing personal finances and making informed investment decisions can be daunting tasks, but AI-powered tools are simplifying the process. They provide insights, recommendations, and strategies to help individuals achieve their financial goals and secure their future.

1. **Wealthfront** (https://www.wealthfront.com): Wealthfront is an automated investment service that uses AI to create and manage personalized portfolios. It considers your financial situation, goals, and risk tolerance to provide a tailored investment strategy.

2. **Betterment** (https://www.betterment.com): Betterment is a robo-advisor that uses AI to create diversified investment portfolios based on your objectives. It continually monitors your investments and rebalances your portfolio to ensure it aligns with your goals.

3. **Personal Capital** (https://www.personalcapital.com): Personal Capital combines AI with human financial advisors. It offers comprehensive financial planning tools and investment tracking. AI analyzes your financial data to provide insights and guidance for optimizing your financial situation.

4. **Mint** (https://mint.intuit.com): Mint is a free personal finance app that uses AI to track and categorize your expenses, create budgets, and provide insights into your

spending habits. It's an excellent tool for gaining a clearer picture of your financial situation.

5. **Yodlee**   (https://www.yodlee.com): Yodlee, owned by Envestnet | Yodlee, provides data aggregation and financial analytics. It allows financial institutions, entrepreneurs, and developers to build applications that help consumers manage their finances.

6. **Acorns**   (https://www.acorns.com): Acorns is an AI-driven micro-investing platform. It rounds up your everyday purchases to the nearest dollar and invests the spare change in a diversified portfolio. It's a simple way to start investing, even if you have limited funds.

7. **Stash** (https://www.stash.com): Stash is an investment app that uses AI to recommend personalized investment strategies based on your financial goals and risk tolerance. It aims to make investing accessible to everyone.

These AI-powered financial tools offer a range of services, from automated investing to budgeting and expense tracking. By leveraging the capabilities of AI, you can take control of your finances, optimize your investments, and work towards achieving your financial objectives. In the sections to follow, we'll explore how AI enhances personal development in other areas, including fitness, mental health, and learning, opening up new possibilities for self-improvement and growth.

Chapter 8: Privacy and Ethics in AI

As AI continues to reshape personal development, from customized fitness and mindfulness applications to language learning and financial guidance, it's crucial to remember that these advancements are accompanied by a pressing need to address ethical concerns, data privacy, and responsible usage. As we transition from the profound impact AI has on personal growth to the multifaceted realm of privacy and ethics, this chapter will guide you through the critical considerations necessary to maintain ethical AI usage and safeguard personal information in this era of unprecedented technological change.

8.1. Understanding AI Ethics and Potential Biases

AI's rapid integration into our daily lives necessitates a deeper understanding of the ethical considerations and potential biases within its algorithms. Promising as it may be, AI also has the capacity to perpetuate or worsen societal biases if not approached with responsibility. In this section, we will delve into the fundamental principles of AI ethics and explore the complexities surrounding potential biases, offering you valuable insights and resources to navigate this intricate terrain.

Key Concepts in AI Ethics

AI ethics revolves around several key principles:

1. *Fairness*: Ensuring that AI systems treat all individuals and groups fairly and without discrimination.

2. *Transparency*: Requiring that AI algorithms are understandable and their decision-making processes explainable.

3. *Privacy*: Protecting user data and ensuring AI systems respect personal privacy.

4. *Accountability*: Establishing clear

responsibility for the outcomes of AI systems.

5. *Safety*: Safeguarding against harm and ensuring the security of AI systems.

6. *Equity*: Addressing the societal impact of AI, striving for equal access and opportunities.

Potential Biases in AI

AI systems can inherit biases from their training data, reflecting historical and societal prejudices. For example:

- *Gender bias*: AI language models have been known to exhibit gender stereotypes in their responses.

- *Racial bias*: Facial recognition technology has been criticized for misidentifying individuals with darker skin tones.

- *Socioeconomic bias*: AI used in lending and hiring can inadvertently favor certain socioeconomic groups.

Addressing AI Ethics and Biases

Several organizations and initiatives aim to address AI ethics and biases:

- *Partnership on AI*: A consortium committed to addressing the global challenges of AI, including ethical concerns. Learn more here: https://partnershiponai.org

- ***Fairness and Machine Learning***: Research and resources on fairness in AI and machine learning. Learn more here: https://fairmlbook.org

- ***AI Now Institute***: A think tank focused on the social implications of AI. Visit the organization here: https://ainowinstitute.org

- ***AI Ethics Lab***: A platform dedicated to AI ethics, offering resources and guidance on the ethical use of artificial intelligence. Learn more here: https://aiethicslab.com

Navigating AI Ethics

Ensuring ethical AI usage involves vigilance and advocacy. Be aware of AI's potential biases, stay informed about evolving ethical guidelines, and promote responsible AI development. It's through collective efforts that AI can be a force for good while mitigating harm.

In the following sections, we'll delve deeper into protecting your data and the regulatory considerations surrounding AI usage, providing you with the knowledge and tools to maintain ethical and responsible AI practices.

8.2. Protecting Your Data in the Age of AI

As AI continues to play a prominent role in our daily lives, the protection of personal data has become a critical concern. AI systems thrive on data, and while they deliver exceptional advantages, they simultaneously raise significant data privacy and security questions. In this section, we will explore strategies to safeguard your data in the AI era, ensuring your digital life remains secure and private. Transitioning from understanding AI ethics and potential biases, we now shift our focus to the practical steps that can be taken to protect your valuable data.

- **Data Encryption:** One fundamental way to protect your data is through encryption. Encryption transforms your data into a code that can only be deciphered by those with the right encryption keys. Messaging apps like WhatsApp and Signal use end-to-end encryption to keep your messages private. Secure email services like ProtonMail provide encrypted email communication, and tools like VeraCrypt allow you to encrypt your files and folders, enhancing the security of your data.

- **Virtual Private Networks (VPNs):** VPNs are essential tools for safeguarding your online privacy. They create a secure and private connection between your device and the internet. NordVPN and ExpressVPN are popular VPN services that anonymize your online presence, making it difficult for prying eyes to track your internet activity.

- **Data Protection Software:** To protect your data from malware and cyber threats, reliable antivirus and anti-malware software is vital. Avast, Norton, and Bitdefender are well-known names in the realm of data protection software, offering comprehensive security suites to keep your devices and data safe.

- **Two-Factor Authentication (2FA):** 2FA adds an extra layer of security to your accounts. It usually involves something you know (password) and something you have (e.g., your smartphone). Google, Facebook, and many other online services offer 2FA options to prevent unauthorized access to your accounts.

- **Privacy-Focused Browsers:** Consider using privacy-focused web browsers like

Mozilla Firefox, Brave, or Tor. These browsers prioritize user privacy, blocking trackers and enhancing your online anonymity.

- **Privacy Tools:** Privacy-focused tools like DuckDuckGo, a search engine that doesn't track your searches, or Privacy Badger, a browser extension that blocks invisible trackers, contribute to a more private online experience.

- **Password Managers:** Using a password manager like LastPass or 1Password helps you create strong, unique passwords for different accounts and stores them securely. This reduces the risk of unauthorized access due to weak or reused passwords.

- **Data Privacy Regulations:** Stay informed about data privacy regulations like the General Data Protection Regulation (GDPR) in the European Union and the California Consumer Privacy Act (CCPA). These regulations provide you with rights and protections related to your personal data.

Resources in the Field:

- *ProtonMail* (https://proton.me/mail) A secure email service that offers end-to-end encryption, ensuring your email communication remains private.

- *NordVPN* (https://nordvpn.com) A trusted VPN service that secures your internet connection, preventing third parties from monitoring your online activity.

- *Bitdefender* (https://www.bitdefender.com) Comprehensive antivirus and cybersecurity software that protects your devices from threats.

- *DuckDuckGo* (https://duckduckgo.com) A privacy-focused search engine that doesn't track your searches.

By adopting these data protection measures and utilizing privacy tools, you can navigate the AI-driven world with confidence, knowing that your data remains under your control and is safeguarded from potential threats. As we move forward in this chapter, we'll explore the regulatory considerations and responsible AI usage, delving into how society can strike a balance between the benefits of AI and individual data protection.

8.3. Regulatory Considerations and Responsible AI Usage

Regulation and responsible usage of AI are

paramount in this technology-advanced era. This section delves into the regulatory considerations surrounding AI and the principles of responsible AI usage. It's crucial to strike a balance between innovation and ethics while ensuring AI aligns with societal norms and values. Let's explore how governments, organizations, and individuals are navigating the intricacies of AI regulation and adopting responsible practices.

- **AI Regulation on a Global Scale:** Governments worldwide are taking steps to regulate AI applications. For instance, the European Union's General Data Protection Regulation (GDPR) governs data privacy and imposes strict requirements on AI systems that process personal data. In the United States, the Federal Trade Commission (FTC) monitors and enforces the use of AI, focusing on consumer protection.

- **Responsible AI Principles:** Leading tech companies are embracing responsible AI practices. Microsoft, for instance, follows six core principles: fairness, reliability and safety, privacy and security, inclusiveness, transparency, and accountability. These principles guide the development and deployment of AI technologies to ensure they align with ethical standards.

- **AI Ethical Frameworks:** Organizations like the Institute of Electrical and Electronics Engineers (IEEE) have established ethical frameworks to promote responsible AI development. The IEEE Global Initiative on Ethics of Autonomous and Intelligent Systems focuses on embedding values and ethical considerations into AI systems.

- **Individual Responsibility:** As AI becomes more accessible, individuals also play a crucial role in responsible AI usage. Understanding privacy settings and data-sharing options on AI-driven platforms is essential. Learning to recognize and report biased, or harmful AI behaviors is another facet of individual responsibility.

Resources in this Field:

- European Union's GDPR: GDPR is a comprehensive regulation that covers data protection, including AI usage. Learn more here: https://gdpr.eu

- Federal Trade Commission (FTC): The FTC regulates AI usage in the United States, focusing on consumer protection. Visit the website here: https://www.ftc.gov/industry/technology/artificial-intelligence

- Microsoft's Responsible AI Principles: Microsoft's principles offer a model for ethical AI development. Learn more here: https://www.microsoft.com/en-us/ai/responsible-ai

- IEEE Global Initiative on Ethics of Autonomous and Intelligent Systems: IEEE's initiative sets ethical standards for AI and autonomous systems. Learn more here: https://standards.ieee.org/initiatives/autonomous-intelligence-systems

- AI Ethics and Bias Reporting: Platforms like Google and Facebook have mechanisms to report AI system bias and harmful content. These mechanisms enable users to actively contribute to responsible AI usage.

Navigating the regulatory environment and embracing responsible AI principles are essential as AI technologies continue to advance. It's a collective effort involving governments, organizations, and individuals to ensure that AI enhances our lives while respecting ethical boundaries. As we delve into the realm of privacy and ethics in AI, we will further explore how these principles can guide us in our AI-driven world.

Chapter 9: The Future of AI

Navigating the future of AI requires a profound understanding of its ethical and privacy considerations, as we've explored in the previous chapter. Now, as we venture into the next chapter, we shift our focus to the limitless potential that AI holds for our world. We'll dive into the emerging trends and groundbreaking innovations, witnessing how AI will influence various facets of our lives. By staying at the forefront of these developments, we can prepare for the AI-driven world of tomorrow, embracing its transformative power and ensuring that we thrive in an ever-evolving technological landscape.

9.1. Emerging Trends and Cutting-Edge AI Innovations

The future of AI is a dynamic and ever-evolving landscape that promises to revolutionize

numerous industries. In this section, we'll delve into the emerging trends and cutting-edge AI innovations that are set to shape our world in the coming years. These innovations span across various sectors, offering solutions to some of our most pressing challenges, from healthcare to transportation and beyond.

- **Healthcare Breakthroughs**: AI is poised to transform healthcare by offering early disease detection, personalized treatment plans, and improving patient care. IBM Watson Health, for instance, applies AI to analyze medical data and assist in diagnosing diseases like cancer. Similarly, PathAI leverages AI to assist pathologists in identifying diseases from medical images.

- **Education and Personalized Learning**: AI will play a pivotal role in education, personalizing learning experiences and expanding access to quality education. Tools like Duolingo, powered by AI, offer language learners an interactive and customized journey. Furthermore, adaptive learning platforms like DreamBox provide students with tailored math lessons, ensuring they grasp concepts at their own pace.

- **Transportation Revolution**: Autonomous vehicles are on the horizon, with companies like Tesla leading the way. These self-driving cars employ AI to navigate and make split-second decisions. They have the potential to reduce accidents, traffic congestion, and offer greater mobility to people with disabilities.

- **Sustainability Solutions**: AI will play a critical role in addressing environmental challenges. For instance, Google's DeepMind uses AI to optimize data center efficiency, leading to significant energy savings. In agriculture, IBM's Watson Decision Platform for Agriculture assists farmers in making data-driven decisions to enhance crop yield and sustainability.

- **Space Exploration and Research**: NASA's Mars rovers, such as Perseverance, use AI to autonomously operate and explore the red planet. AI is also used to analyze vast datasets from space telescopes, aiding in the discovery of exoplanets and unraveling the mysteries of the universe.

- **Innovations in AI Hardware**: AI advancements are not limited to software; hardware innovations are equally significant. Companies like NVIDIA develop powerful GPUs that accelerate AI computations. Quantum computing is also on the horizon, which promises to revolutionize AI capabilities.

- **Quantum AI**: In the future, AI will get a significant boost from quantum computing. This means AI systems will be much more powerful and able to handle extremely complex tasks much faster than before. We're talking about ultra-accurate simulations, faster drug discoveries, and AI that's smarter than ever.

- **Brain-Computer Interfaces (BCIs)**: In the coming years, we'll see the rise of BCIs. These are technologies that connect your brain directly to computers, allowing you to control them just by thinking. It's an exciting innovation with huge potential in healthcare, particularly for people with disabilities. However, it also raises important questions about privacy and control. BCIs will revolutionize how we interact with AI and how we understand our own brains.

- **Robotics and Automation**: Robotics combined with AI is set to revolutionize numerous industries, making processes more efficient and reducing the need for human intervention. From manufacturing and logistics to healthcare and agriculture, AI-driven robots are taking on tasks that were once manual and time-consuming. This trend promises to increase productivity and reshape job roles in the workforce.

These examples provide a glimpse of how AI will drive innovation in the future, transforming industries and enhancing our daily lives. As we explore these exciting advancements, remember that staying informed about AI trends will be key to embracing the opportunities they offer and adapting to the AI-driven world of tomorrow.

9.2. Preparing for the AI-Driven World of Tomorrow

As AI continues to advance and integrate into various aspects of our lives, it becomes increasingly essential to prepare for this AI-driven world of tomorrow. Understanding the capabilities, limitations, and potential impacts of AI is crucial, and equipping yourself with the knowledge and skills to navigate this evolving landscape will be invaluable.

- **AI Education and Training**: To prepare for the AI-driven future, consider enrolling in online courses and programs that focus on AI and machine learning.

Platforms like Coursera and edX offer a range of courses, including Stanford University's Machine Learning and Deep Learning Specializations. Learning these skills will not only help you understand AI but also potentially open new career opportunities.

- **Ethical AI and Bias Mitigation**: With the proliferation of AI comes the need to understand and address ethical concerns and potential biases in AI systems. Resources like the Responsible AI toolkit from Microsoft provide insights into building and deploying AI systems responsibly. Additionally, staying informed about AI ethics and developments in bias mitigation is essential.

- **AI in the Workplace**: As AI becomes more prevalent in the workplace, understanding how to work alongside AI systems and even supervising them is a valuable skill. Familiarize yourself with AI tools commonly used in your industry, and explore how they can enhance your productivity. For example, customer support roles often use chatbots to handle routine inquiries, allowing human agents to focus on complex issues.

- **Privacy and Data Protection**: As AI relies on data, safeguarding your personal information is crucial. Familiarize yourself with data privacy laws and practices, such as the General Data Protection Regulation (GDPR) in the European Union. Tools like virtual private networks (VPNs) and end-to-end encryption can help protect your data.

- **AI and Creativity**: AI's influence is extending into creative fields, including art and music. Embrace AI as a creative tool, and explore how it can complement your artistic endeavors. Platforms like Amper Music and Runway ML provide AI-powered creative tools.

- **Continuous Learning**: AI evolves rapidly, so maintaining a learning mindset is essential. Subscribe to AI-related journals, follow AI news outlets, and participate in AI communities and forums to stay updated with the latest advancements.

- **Collaboration and Innovation**: Explore opportunities for collaboration and innovation in your field. AI can enhance research, product development, and customer experiences. Consider partnerships with AI experts and explore how AI can drive innovation in your domain.

- **Global Awareness**: AI is a global phenomenon with diverse applications worldwide. Staying informed about international AI trends and global AI ethics is important for individuals and businesses alike.

By preparing for the AI-driven world of tomorrow, you'll not only stay ahead of the curve but also contribute to shaping a future where AI serves as a powerful tool for improving the quality of life and solving some of our most significant challenges. Transitioning from an observer to an active participant in the AI landscape will be a rewarding journey that positions you for success in the AI-powered world ahead.

Chapter 10: Building Your Own AI Projects

As we conclude this exploration of AI's present and future, it's important to emphasize that AI is not just a subject of study, but a realm of active participation. In the AI-driven world of tomorrow, the power to create, innovate, and shape the future lies within your reach. This final chapter empowers you to embark on your AI creation journey, providing insights into the exciting world of coding and development with AI. You'll explore an introduction to AI programming languages, discover invaluable resources for learning, and receive essential tips for launching your AI projects. It's time to transform your AI dreams into reality and create your own AI-driven innovations.

10.1. Introduction to Coding and Development with AI

Begin your journey to create AI-driven projects is an exciting endeavor. To get started, you'll need to familiarize yourself with the basics of coding and development in the context of artificial intelligence. Don't worry if you're not a coding expert; AI development has become increasingly accessible, even for those without extensive technical backgrounds.

Getting Started with AI Coding

1. *Python*: *The Language of AI*: Python is the go-to programming language for AI. It's known for its simplicity, readability, and extensive library ecosystem tailored for AI and machine learning. You can start your

coding journey by learning Python from resources like Python.org. Learn more here: https://www.python.org

- ***AI Frameworks and Libraries***: AI development often involves the use of frameworks and libraries. TensorFlow (https://www.tensorflow.org), PyTorch (https://pytorch.org), and scikit-learn (https://scikit-learn.org/stable/index.html) are popular choices. These resources offer tutorials and documentation to help you get started.

Online Courses and Tutorials

1. ***Coursera***: Coursera offers a wide range of AI and machine learning courses, including the renowned "Machine Learning" course by Andrew Ng. This platform is a great resource to deepen your understanding of AI concepts.

2. ***edX***: edX provides courses from top universities like MIT and Harvard. Their AI and machine learning courses are comprehensive and accessible to learners of all levels.

AI Development Environments

1. ***Jupyter Notebook***: Jupyter Notebook is an open-source web application that allows

you to create and share documents that contain live code, equations, visualizations, and narrative text. It's an excellent tool for AI development, and you can get started by following the Jupyter documentation.

2. ***Google Colab***: Google Colab is a cloud-based Jupyter Notebook that offers free GPU support. It's a fantastic resource for AI projects, and you can access it through your Google account.

Books and Learning Resources

- ***"Python for Data Analysis" by Wes McKinney***: This book is an excellent resource for learning Python for data science and AI.

- ***"Deep Learning" by Ian Goodfellow, Yoshua Bengio, and Aaron Courville***: For a deep dive into AI, this book provides comprehensive insights into deep learning techniques.

Community and Forums

- ***Stack Overflow***: When you encounter coding challenges or have questions, Stack Overflow is a go-to platform where you can find answers and seek help from the coding community.

- ***GitHub***: GitHub is a hub for AI projects and code repositories. You can explore existing projects, collaborate, and learn from the codebase of AI developers worldwide.

AI Project Ideas

1. ***Image Recognition***: Develop an image recognition model that can identify objects or scenes in photos.

2. ***Chatbot***: Create a conversational AI chatbot for websites or messaging platforms.

3. ***Predictive Analytics***: Build a predictive model for stock market trends, weather forecasts, or other data-driven predictions.

Remember, AI development is a journey that involves continuous learning and experimentation. Don't be afraid to make mistakes and iterate on your projects. With these foundational resources and a curious mindset, you'll be well on your way to bringing your AI project ideas to life.

10.2. Resources for Learning AI Programming Languages

Learning programming languages for artificial intelligence (AI) is a crucial step in your

journey to create AI-driven projects. Fortunately, there are abundant resources available to help you master the languages essential for AI development. Here, we'll explore some of the key programming languages for AI and the resources to learn them.

1. Python: The AI Powerhouse

Python is the predominant language for AI and machine learning due to its simplicity and rich library ecosystem. Resources for learning Python include:

- Python.org: The official Python website provides extensive documentation, tutorials, and the Python Software Foundation's (PSF) learning resources.

- Coursera's "Python for Everybody": This course is a great introduction to Python for beginners and offers valuable insights into how to apply Python in AI projects.

2. R: A Language for Data Analysis and Visualization

R is widely used for data analysis and visualization in AI. Learning resources for R include:

- R Project for Statistical Computing:

The official website offers comprehensive documentation and tutorials for mastering R.

- edX's "Data Science MicroMasters": This program includes R programming courses and is an excellent choice for in-depth learning.

3. Julia: A High-Performance AI Language

Julia is gaining prominence for its high performance in numerical and scientific computing. Learn Julia through:

- The Julia Programming Language: The official website provides resources, documentation, and tutorials for mastering Julia.

- Coursera's "Julia Scientific Programming": This course offers insights into using Julia for scientific and AI applications.

4. Java: AI for Android Apps

Java is essential for AI development in Android apps. Resources for learning Java include:

- Oracle's Java Documentation: The official source for Java resources and documentation.

- Udemy's "Complete Java Masterclass": This

course is an excellent starting point for Java beginners.

5. C++: High-Performance AI

C++ is favored for AI projects requiring high performance. Learn C++ through:

- cplusplus.com: A valuable resource for C++ tutorials and documentation.

- edX's "C++ Programming": This course provides insights into mastering C++ for AI and other applications.

6. Prolog: AI Logic Programming

Prolog is a logic programming language commonly used in AI. Resources for learning Prolog include:

- **Learn Prolog Now!**: This online book offers a comprehensive guide to Prolog.

- **edX's "Artificial Intelligence"**: This course provides an introduction to Prolog for AI applications.

7. JavaScript: AI in Web Development

JavaScript is essential for AI in web development. Learn JavaScript through:

- *MDN Web Docs*: The Mozilla Developer Network offers extensive documentation and tutorials for JavaScript.

- ***Coursera's "HTML, CSS, and JavaScript"***: This course is ideal for beginners looking to learn JavaScript for web-based AI.

8. Swift: AI in iOS Development

Swift is used for AI projects on iOS devices. Resources for learning Swift include:

- ***Swift.org***: The official Swift website provides documentation and tutorials.

- ***Udemy's "iOS 14 & Swift 5 - The Complete iOS App Development Course"***: This course is ideal for learning Swift for iOS AI applications.

These programming languages serve different AI purposes, so choose the one that aligns with your project goals. Consider taking online courses, exploring official documentation, and engaging with coding communities to deepen your language skills for AI development.

10.3. Tips for Starting Your AI Project

Embarking on your AI project is an exciting endeavor. However, the complexity of artificial intelligence can be overwhelming for beginners. Here, we provide valuable tips to help you start your AI project with confidence and efficiency.

1. **Define Your Project Goals:** Before you start coding, you must have a clear understanding of your project's objectives. Define what you want to achieve with your AI application. Whether it's image recognition, natural language processing, or something else, clarity on your goals is essential.

2. **Choose the Right Tools and Libraries:** Selecting the right tools and libraries is crucial. Python, with libraries like TensorFlow, PyTorch, and scikit-learn, is a versatile choice for many AI projects. Ensure you have the necessary software and packages installed.

3. **Learn the Basics:** Understanding AI fundamentals is essential. Study concepts such as machine learning, deep learning, neural networks, and data preprocessing. Online courses, books, and tutorials can be valuable resources.

4. **Data Collection and Preparation:** Data is the lifeblood of AI projects. Gather, clean, and preprocess your data meticulously. Tools like Python's pandas library are

useful for data manipulation.

5. **Explore Pre-trained Models:** To save time, consider using pre-trained AI models. These models are trained on large datasets and can be fine-tuned for your specific task. Platforms like Hugging Face Transformers offer a wide array of pre-trained models.

6. **Start Small:** Begin with a manageable scope. Create a Minimum Viable Product (MVP) to test your project's feasibility. Once it's working, you can expand and add complexity.

7. **Debugging and Testing:** Expect to encounter bugs and challenges. Debugging is a significant part of AI development. Use debugging tools and testing frameworks to ensure your project's reliability.

8. **Collaborate and Seek Help:** Don't hesitate to seek help and collaborate with others. Online communities like Stack Overflow, GitHub, and Reddit are excellent resources for finding solutions to common AI issues.

9. **Document Your Work:** Keep thorough documentation of your project, including code comments, explanations,

and records of experiments. This documentation is invaluable for future reference and sharing your work.

10. **Stay Updated:** The field of AI is dynamic, with frequent advancements. Stay updated with the latest research papers, blogs, and AI news. This knowledge will help you implement the most recent techniques in your project.

11. **Ethical Considerations:** Consider the ethical implications of your AI project. Be conscious of potential biases in your data and ensure your project adheres to ethical guidelines.

12. **Share Your Work:** Open sourcing your AI project on platforms like GitHub allows you to receive feedback, collaborate with others, and showcase your skills to potential employers.

13. **Continuous Learning:** AI is a continuous learning journey. As you complete your project, take the opportunity to learn from your experiences, reflect on your mistakes, and plan your next AI venture.

With these tips, you're well-equipped to begin your AI project. Remember that AI development is a dynamic field, and patience, persistence, and a willingness to learn are your greatest assets. Enjoy your AI journey!

Conclusion

As we conclude this book, we find ourselves at a unique juncture in human history. The rise of artificial intelligence has ushered in an era of unprecedented transformation, touching every facet of our lives. We've embarked on a journey through the realms of AI, exploring its applications across diverse domains. From understanding the fundamentals of AI to witnessing its impact on creativity, entertainment, personal development, and ethical considerations, we've navigated the AI landscape together.

Embracing the AI-Driven Future

The future is AI-driven, and rather than fearing the unknown, we must embrace it with open minds and open hearts. AI is a powerful tool that has the potential to uplift humanity in countless ways. It can augment our capabilities, improve efficiency, and enable us to solve complex challenges. The stories of AI-driven success are growing by the day, from healthcare breakthroughs to innovations in transportation and beyond. As we embrace this AI-driven future, we step into a world brimming with opportunities.

Transforming Your Life with AI

In this journey, we've seen how AI can transform your life. It can aid in your personal fitness journey, empower your mental well-being, help you learn new languages, guide your financial decisions, and inspire you to embark on your own AI projects. AI isn't just a concept; it's a practical, everyday tool that can elevate your life in profound ways.

The Journey Ahead: Stay Informed and Empowered

As AI continues to evolve, it's crucial to stay informed and empowered. The field of artificial intelligence is dynamic and ever-changing. It's not just for data scientists and programmers; it's for everyone who is curious and open to learning. AI has the potential to be a great equalizer, opening doors to new skills, opportunities, and innovative thinking.

The journey doesn't end with this book. It's only the beginning. AI is a lifelong adventure, and the more you explore, the more you will discover. Whether you're a student, professional, or simply someone intrigued by the possibilities, AI is a companion in your journey of personal and societal growth.

In this AI-driven future, our responsibility is not just to use AI, but to use it wisely and ethically.

Together, we must shape the AI landscape to reflect our values, ensuring it benefits all of humanity.

Remember, the future belongs to those who are informed, adaptable, and ready to embrace the ever-evolving world of AI. The journey ahead is thrilling, and it's yours to embark upon.

So, stay curious, stay informed, and stay empowered. The AI-driven world of tomorrow is yours to explore, shape, and thrive in.

Glossary

1. Algorithm: A set of rules and instructions used to solve a specific problem or perform a particular task within AI and machine learning.

2. AI (Artificial Intelligence): The simulation of human intelligence processes by machines, including learning, reasoning, problem-solving, and decision-making.

3. Automation: The use of AI and machines to perform tasks with minimal human intervention, often in manufacturing, logistics, and customer service

4. Big Data: Large datasets with varying formats, are often used for training AI models and extracting valuable insights.

5. Chatbot: A computer program designed to simulate human conversation, often used for customer service and virtual assistance.

6. Data Science: The interdisciplinary field of extracting knowledge and insights from structured and unstructured data, often involving AI and machine learning techniques.

7. Deep Learning: A subset of machine

learning using deep neural networks with multiple layers to analyze and make predictions from vast datasets.

8. Ethical AI: The practice of developing and using AI systems that adhere to ethical principles and guidelines, ensuring fairness, transparency, and human rights.

9. Fintech: The use of AI, machine learning, and technology to enhance financial services, including digital banking and cryptocurrencies.

10. HealthTech: The application of AI and technology to improve healthcare, including diagnostics, treatment, and telemedicine.

11. Human-AI Collaboration: The synergy between human intelligence and AI systems to improve productivity, problem-solving, and decision-making.

12. Machine Learning: A subset of AI that allows systems to automatically learn and improve from experience without being explicitly programmed.

13. Neural Network: A system of algorithms designed to recognize patterns, used in deep learning and various AI tasks.

14. Personalization: The use of AI to

customize products, content, and experiences based on an individual's preferences and behaviors.

15. Quantum Computing: A field of study involving the use of quantum-mechanical phenomena to perform computation, with potential applications in AI.

16. Transfer Learning: A machine learning technique that allows AI models to apply knowledge from one domain to another, reducing the need for extensive training data.

17. Unstructured Data: Data that lacks a predefined structure, often textual or visual in nature, and requires advanced AI techniques for analysis.

18. Virtual Reality (VR): Technology that creates a simulated environment, allowing users to interact with a computer-generated world.

19. Bias in AI: Unfair or discriminatory outcomes in AI systems that can result from biased data or algorithms.

20. Data Labeling: The process of tagging or annotating data to train machine learning models, often used in supervised learning.

21. Hardware Acceleration: The use of specialized hardware, like GPUs and TPUs, to speed up AI and machine learning computations.

22. Intelligent Process Automation (IPA): The use of AI and automation to streamline business processes, often in finance and HR.

23. Jupyter Notebook: An open-source web application used for creating and sharing documents with live code, equations, and visualizations.

24. Precision and Recall: Metrics used to evaluate the performance of classification models.

25. Quantum AI: A field exploring the potential of quantum computing in AI, promising breakthroughs in solving complex problems and optimizing AI models.

26. Recommender System: AI applications that provide personalized recommendations, commonly used in e-commerce and content platforms.

27. Self-Supervised Learning: A type of unsupervised learning where AI models learn from unlabeled data, often used in

pretraining models.

28. Unsupervised Learning: A type of machine learning where AI systems learn patterns and structures in data without labeled output.

29. Virtual Assistant: AI-driven programs designed to provide assistance and perform tasks for users, such as Siri, Alexa, and Google Assistant.

ABOUT THE AUTHOR

Bo Zhang

Ed.D., is an educator, researcher, and writer. Bo is the co-editor of the book Crossing Borders, Bridging Cultures: The Narratives of Global Scholars, and currently serves in varying capacities for the American Educational Research Association, TESOL International Association, NAFSA, and International Association of Student Affairs and Services. Bo also serves as a reviewer for the Journal of Interdisciplinary Studies in Education and the Journal of Learning and Instruction